East S

A DOG WALKER'S GUIDE

David and Hilary Staines

COUNTRYSIDE BOOKS
NEWBURY BERKSHIRE

Countryside Books
3 Catherine Road
Newbury
Berkshire
RG14 7NA

To view our complete range of books please visit us at
www.countrysidebooks.co.uk

First published 2016
© Text and Photographs 2016 David and Hilary Staines

A CIP record for this book is available from the British Library.

ISBN 978 1 84674 337 5

Produced by The Letterworks Ltd., Reading
Typeset by KT Designs, St Helens
Printed by Gomer Press, Llandysul, Ceredigion

Contents

Walk

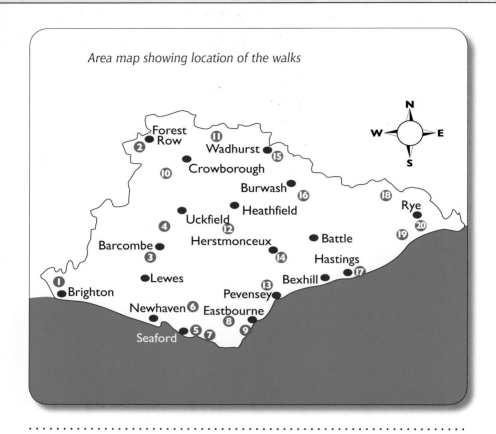

Area map showing location of the walks

PUBLISHER'S NOTE

We hope that you obtain considerable enjoyment from this book; great care has been taken in its preparation. Although at the time of publication all routes followed public rights of way or permitted paths, diversion orders can be made and permissions withdrawn.

We cannot, of course, be held responsible for such diversion orders and any inaccuracies in the text which result from these or any other changes to the routes nor any damage which might result from walkers trespassing on private property. We are anxious though that all details covering the walks are kept up to date and would therefore welcome information from readers which would be relevant to future editions.

The simple sketch maps that accompany the walks in this book are based on notes made by the author whilst checking out the routes on the ground. They are designed to show you how to reach the start, to point out the main features of the overall circuit and they contain a progression of numbers that relate to the paragraphs of the text.

However, for the benefit of a proper map, we do recommend that you purchase the relevant Ordnance Survey sheet covering your walk. The Ordnance Survey maps are widely available, especially through booksellers and local newsagents.

INTRODUCTION

Welcome to this dog walker's guide to East Sussex. There are few counties in England that can match the variety of scenery and history here. From the rolling hills of the High Weald to stunning coastal scenery where the South Downs meet the English Channel, East Sussex is a county of striking contrast. On these 20 circular walks, you can explore its charming landscape dotted with picturesque towns and villages, wide open marshes, beaches and majestic cliff top coastlines. You are sure to be delighted with its variety and beauty, and of course your 'faithful friend' will be enthralled by the vast expanse of nature's finest to explore.

A large part of the stunning South Downs National Park lies within the county, and the walks between Brighton and Eastbourne have been specifically chosen to cover this area. But there is so much to see and do at just about every turn in the Sussex countryside. We have incorporated places of history and interest into the walks, including a steam railway, castles and an old observatory, so as to make them interesting for you, as well as your dog. With this book, your companion will always enjoy a great time out, and so will you.

Each of the walks has been specially surveyed for dog walkers. A wider range of cafés and pubs now allow dogs through their doors and we've recommended a refreshment spot for each walk. We've also listed the nearest vets, any livestock you might encounter, as well as handy parking information.

We have found the occasional dog passage through or around stiles to have been deliberately blocked up and have had to find alternative paths for you. If you find your route obstructed in any way, do not risk harming your animal by forcing them through or over the stile. If in any doubt, or where a path has become unclear, always be prepared to turn round and just retrace your steps back to the starting place. It's also a good idea to bring the relevant Ordnance Survey map with you – we always give details of the relevant sheet as part of the walk.

We are sure you will enjoy walking with your dog in the East Sussex countryside!

David and Hilary Staines

ADVICE FOR DOG WALKERS

The **Countryside Code** has published six steps to ensure walking your dog in the countryside is as safe as possible. These are:

1 Control your dog so that it does not scare or disturb farm animals or wildlife.
2 When using new access rights over open country and common land you must keep your dog on a short lead between 1 March and 31 July – and all year round near farm animals – and you may not be able to take your dog at all on some areas or at some times. Please follow any official signs.
3 You do not have to put your dog on a lead on public paths, as long as it is under close control. But as a general rule, keep your dog on a lead if you cannot rely on its obedience. By law farmers are entitled to destroy a dog that injures or worries their animals.
4 If a farm animal chases you and your dog, it is safer to let your dog off the lead – don't risk getting hurt by trying to protect it.
5 Take particular care that your dog doesn't scare sheep or lambs, or wander where it might disturb birds that nest on the ground and other wildlife – eggs and young will soon die without protection from their parents.
6 Everyone knows how unpleasant dog mess is and it can cause infections, so always clean up after your dog and get rid of the mess responsibly. Also make sure your dog is wormed regularly to protect it, other animals and people.

Dogs can suffer from heat stroke in hot weather, or if left shut in cars. They will pant excessively and may vomit, collapse, have fits or difficulty breathing. If heat stroke occurs:

1 Keep the dog calm. Move it into the shade, a cool building or room, or near a fan or breeze.
2 Cool all of your dog with water, paying particular attention to the head.
3 Let your dog drink small amounts of cool water frequently.
4 Call a vet.

Finally, check your dog for ticks after a walk, especially if you've been through a wooded area or near bracken. If you find a tick, remove it straight away with tweezers, or better still a special tick remover from the vets.

Well, that's the serious bit out of the way. Now it's time to enjoy a guided doggie roam around some of the best places in England for walking your dog.

Brighton's Chattri Memorial and the South Downs

The Chattri memorial, 500 feet above the city of Brighton.

This is a walk that takes you to one of the most remarkable features in the entire county. Hidden away high on the side of the South Downs only a few miles from the bustle of Brighton, the Chattri memorial is a place few people have ever heard of. Yet it is a place of great symbolism with a fascinating and proud history. This walk takes you to this scenic part of the downs, 500 feet above Brighton.

Terrain

Quiet country lanes, footpaths and crossing 'open access' downland. This walk involves an energetic and fairly steep climb at the start. We encountered sheep, cattle and horses. In fields with livestock, always keep dogs on a lead.

Where to park

There are official parking places on Braypool Lane to the north and slightly east of the Patcham exit off the A27. **Grid Ref**: TQ 302094. **Map**: OS Explorer 122 Brighton and Hove.

How to get there

Following the A23 into Brighton take the A27 exit towards Lewes. Having skirted the main Mill Road roundabout, at the second small roundabout follow the A27 Lewes lane but take the second exit onto the minor road. This is Braypool Lane. Then turn sharp right, there is official roadside parking a few yards further on. **Sat Nav**: BN1 8YF.

Refreshments

Although this walk is so close to Brighton, you are off the tourist trail and there are no pubs or cafés on the route. But it's the perfect spot for a picnic and to enjoy the peace and tranquillity. Alternatively, Stanmer Park Tea Rooms off the A27 welcomes dogs inside and out and is open 7 days a week.

Dog factors

Distance: 2½ miles.
Road walking: At the start of the walk along a very quiet lane.
Livestock: The potential for a wide variety of livestock. We used a long retractable lead for this walk.
Stiles: None
Nearest vets: Top Cat Veterinary Centre, 146 Mackie Avenue, Brighton BN1 8SB. ☎ 01273 504800

The Walk

1 With your back to the main road take the lane that heads directly uphill, away from the main road. Follow the lane for about 1/3 mile. After it drops down and takes a right hand bend there are some livestock pens on the left hand side of the road. Immediately after the pens there is a gate and public footpath sign.

2 Go through the gate. As the council notice on the gate states, this is open access land. You are heading for the **Chattri Memorial** which you can clearly see on the hillside in front of and above you. Cross the field in the direction of the memorial but keep to the left of the wooded area in front of you. Keep skirting this area around to the left and do not drop down into the valley. Keep climbing uphill all the way round, still keeping the tree line on your right. After you have reached the level of the memorial you will see some gates in the enclosure. Go through either of them into the grounds of the memorial.

Around 800,000 Indian soldiers fought for Britain in the First World War. Some of those injured were hospitalised in a variety of locations around Brighton. In 1915, the bodies of 53 Hindu and Sikh men who had died from their injuries were taken to this remote spot and in accordance with religious custom a funeral pyre (or ghat) was built for their cremation and the ashes subsequently scattered in the sea. A permanent memorial to the men was then promoted. The Chattri was designed by a young Indian architect from Bombay and was unveiled by the Prince of Wales in 1921.

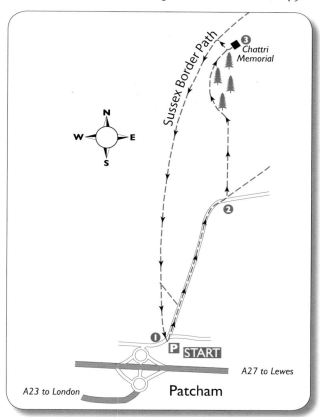

3 Return out of the gate you entered then turn sharp right alongside the fence line and walk a short distance up to the path close to the top of the hill. Turn left onto the path. You now follow this all the way down the hill. After a mile, keeping going in the same direction, you will return back to the start of the walk.

2

Forest Row

The stark towers of ruined Brambletye House. These were once linked to form a continual frontage to the mansion.

This is a walk at the far west end of the county, centred on an historic village. Forest Row grew from a medieval hamlet into a prosperous village on the main London – Lewes Road. There is plenty of open countryside to enjoy and the walk passes a striking ruin of a Jacobean mansion. Brambletye House was built in the reign of James I but was abandoned early in its life. Today three stone towers stand in memory of a disgraced owner. It dates from 1631 and was built for local MP Sir Henry Compton. Its second owner was accused of treason and fled to Spain to live in exile. It seems the house never recovered. It remained unoccupied thereafter and fell into ruin.

Terrain

Paths and quiet country lanes. The paths can be particularly muddy in winter. There is a little road walking in the village centre and the main A22 is busy. The lanes away from the village (after you have crossed the A22 on the walk)

Dog factors

Distance: 3 miles.
Road walking: Mostly paths, some quiet country lanes but busier roads in the village centre.
Livestock: None encountered.
Stiles: Many, but all dog friendly with a variety of ways through.
Nearest vets: Forest Lodge Veterinary Centre, Station Road, Forest Row RH18 5DW ☎ 01342 824452 (between points 1 and 2 on the walk)

are all very quiet and we felt comfortable with the dog off lead, although of course use your own judgement in relation to both your own animal and prevailing traffic when you visit.

Where to park

Forest Row village, Lower Road car park. It is to the rear of the Foresters Arms public house off Hartfield Road. The car park is divided into short stay (3 hours maximum) and long stay, so be careful which part you use if you intend an extended visit. If full, there is another car park slightly further down Hartfield Road. **Grid Ref**: TQ 427348. **Map**: OS Explorer 135 Ashdown Forest.

How to get there

From the M25 take Junction 6, A22 signposted towards Eastbourne. Be careful to follow the A22 signs through East Grinstead town centre. Once you arrive in Forest Row, at the roundabout in front of the church turn left, following the car parking signs. Turn left into Station Road and immediately left again into Lower Road. You will see the car park if you follow the signs in any event. **Sat Nav**: RH18 5HE.

Refreshments

Refreshments are available from Forest Row Cycle Hire Centre which is located in the Bike Shop in Lower Road car park at the very start of the walk.

The **Chequers Inn**, after point 5 on the walk, dates from 1452 and allows dogs in the atmospheric low ceilinged bar. It's an archetypal old English inn complete with roaring fire in the inglenook fireplace. The bar is usually open all day. ☎ 01342 823333.

For convenience food there is a Tesco Express in the village centre opposite the Chequers and a Co-op in the parade of shops on the right hand side of Hartfield Road close to the car park.

The Walk

1 Turn left out of **Lower Road car park** down **Station Road**. At the end when you are facing the village club and fire station bear right keeping the fire station and recycling yard on your left. Walk along to the gate at the end and turn sharp left onto the **Forest Way**. Keep the scout hut on your left as the path rises up an incline and emerges out onto a quiet lane. Turn left and keep going along the lane. You will pass the vets on the left and the old waterworks on your right. Be careful as the lane will finish at the busy A22 which you cross at the pedestrian traffic lights. Keep going in the same direction now on the path which forms the Forest Way again and now climbs slightly onto the course of an old railway line.

2 Keep going until you come across the first lane that crosses the path. This was **Brambletye Crossing** and the house on the left hand side, although now much enlarged, was once the railway level crossing keeper's cottage. Turn left off the path and follow the lane. Soon the towers of **Brambletye House** loom up on your left. Take a few minutes to take in this curious sight.

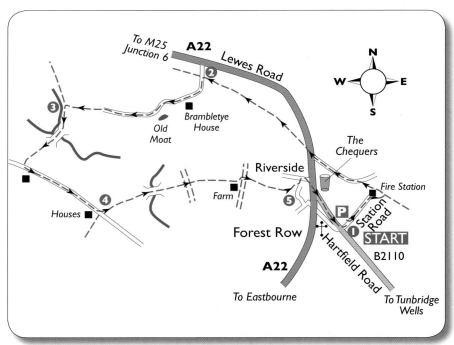

Brambletye House is unusual, as a grand house it fell to ruin early in its life after its owner fled the country accused of treason in 1693. It is said that he was hunting in the Ashdown Forest when warned that his accusers were searching the house. He rode straight to the coast and took a boat to Spain. It is claimed that no other owner ever passed through the gatehouse again. By the mid 18th century it was a ruin with parts of its stone work robbed for use in building work elsewhere. The last habitable part was the gatehouse. Surprisingly the ruin has survived intact over the centuries. In one of the three-storey towers some of the original glass is still in place in the windows. By the 20th century the remains were completely covered in trees and ivy which was cleared away in 1930. Since 2009 it has been on Historic England's 'At Risk' register due to its general deterioration. The towers are all on private land and are inaccessible but there is a fine view from the walk. The remains of the gate house are right next to the path so you can have a closer look.

Time to practise the Sit and Stay command!

Keep following the lane in the same direction and follow its twists and turns. On your left you may notice the remains of a medieval moat which still contains water in wet weather. Where the lane peters out with a farmyard on the right keep going ahead up the path which rises up a slight incline. Be very careful here as a live electric fence on the right hand side protects the poultry farm behind it. Very soon the path tops the incline and you need to immediately take a dog-leg left along the signed path. This turn can be a bit hidden in summer.

3 The path is narrow and to the right falls away quite steeply towards a stream. Keep going over a footbridge, the path now bears slightly left across the field. Follow the path over the stile at the end. For a short distance it runs next to a lane, this is the private service road to **Weir Wood Reservoir**. At the end of the path, continue along the lane in the same direction. As soon as you pass some houses on the right hand side, take the path on the left.

4 The path follows the left hand hedgerow, keep going to the end, cross the stream and go through the gate. Keep following the path in the same direction. Continue in the same direction where the path is crossed by a trackway. Follow the yellow waymarkers and keep on in the same direction once you have crossed the trackway. At the following stile the path bears slightly right and crosses a field. You need to head to the left of the house on the hillside. Cross the stile and head up the track a short distance. Follow the footpath sign left, avoiding the farmyard. At the stile, turn sharp right and at the fence that is now facing you, cross the stile and the lane and keep going ahead through the gate which is facing you in the tree line, again following the yellow waymarkers. Keep the hedgerow to your left and at the end cross the stile in the tree line. Now follow the path as it drops down towards the road.

5 The path will become pebble lined as it nears the houses. Where it emerges onto a private car park turn sharp left across the car park and at the road turn right, with the hotel on your right hand side. When you come out onto the main road in the village centre turn right. The **Chequers Inn** is on your left across the road. You need to cross the road and head up the slip road next to the inn marked with 'no entry' signs for vehicles. There are pedestrian lights across the main road a little further along. At the end of the slip road turn left into **Hartfield Road**. The car park and starting point are a short way down on the left hand side.

3

Barcombe Mills

Walking alongside one of the many water channels at Barcombe Mills.

This is a pleasant and popular walking area and takes in the streams and tributaries that flow into the River Ouse. Barcombe Mills was once a small centre of industry with mills and even a button factory that relied on water to power machinery. Industry here is now long gone, but its legacy of man-made water channels, mill streams, sluices and weirs remains.

Terrain

This walk is all on the level using footpaths, tracks and bridleways and is completely dog friendly. A lot of the paths are by watercourses and can get muddy at times.

Where to park

There is a free car park on Barcombe Mills Road just before you reach Barcombe Mills. **Grid Ref**: TQ 433147. **Map**: OS Explorer 122 Brighton and Hove.

East Sussex – A Dog Walker's Guide

How to get there

From the A26 Uckfield to Lewes Road take the turn signposted for Barcombe Cross, this is about three miles north of Lewes. The car park is clearly signposted on the right hand side, about ½ a mile along the lane. **Sat Nav**: BN8 5BP.

Refreshments

The Royal Oak in Barcombe Cross is a mile further on along the lane from the car park. At the crossroads in the centre of the village, turn left. Dogs are welcome. Food is available Monday to Saturday 12 – 3 pm and 6 pm – 8.45 pm, Sundays and Bank Holidays 12 – 3 pm only. The pub even features its own skittle alley. ☎ 01273 400418. At point 3 the walk passes the Anchor Inn. See the Isfield walk for details.

Dog factors
. . . .

Distance: 2½ miles.
Road walking: Two very short distances of a few hundred yards.
Livestock: There may be ground-nesting waterfowl depending on the time of year. Please heed any notices to put dogs on leads where necessary.
Stiles: A few.
Nearest vets: Coastway Vets, 137 Malling Street, Lewes BN7 2RB.
☎ 01273 478100

The Walk
. . . .

1 From **Barcombe Mills parish car park** take the footpath at the far end of the car park. This is to the left if you have your back to the road. Continue along the lane. Just before the second bridge take the footpath marked '**Ouse Valley Way**', with the yellow marker pointing to the right, away from the lane. The Ouse Valley Way has split here so ignore the sign with the white marker. Carry on along the footpath with the stream and the weir to your left. Continue along the footpath keeping the river to your left and cross the stream by the footbridge. Follow the path over the field and through the gate at the end. Keep going along the river bank as the footpath passes over another footbridge. For a short while you will have a watercourse on both sides of the path.

2 The path soon emerges onto a field. You are heading for the buildings in the distance. In front of the buildings, cross the river over the bridge and at the gate at the other side turn right along the track. Follow the track around the open area and take the footpath waymarked through the trees. Continue, passing the brick and concrete Second World War pillbox.

This pillbox dates from around 1940. Structures such as this were built to form defensive lines which utilised existing natural obstacles in order to slow down any invading force. In this case, the natural obstacle is the adjacent River Ouse. There could have been be no realistic suggestion that a few defenders holed up with only

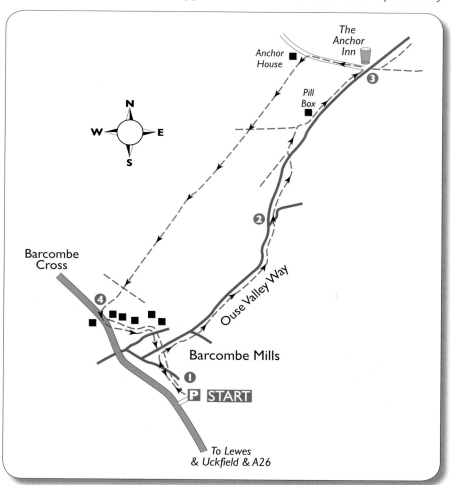

machine guns to hand would have had any chance of survival when faced with the might of the advancing mechanised German army.

After the pillbox go through the gate, keeping the stream on your right. Carry on until you get to the **Anchor Inn**.

3 In front of the pub turn left along the lane. Just before **Anchor House** take the left hand turn along the bridleway. Continue along the bridleway for a mile.

4 Where a road crosses the bridleway, turn left and then bear left down the side lane. Where the lane ends turn right through the gate and follow the old road over the bridge.

This is the site of the original mill. Milling here dates back to the 11th century. The course of the river still reflects some of the artificial channels dug to divert the flow of the water through wheels to power the mills. The last big mill here was built in 1870 and burnt down in 1939. With the mills gone, the once thriving community shrank to just a handful of houses. The old road that you are walking along passed by some of the buildings. Tolls were levied to cross the bridges over the river. The charging of tolls here featured in the Domesday Book, commissioned by William the Conqueror. The modern road has now been diverted around the site.

Carry on and you will soon be on your outward route back to the car park.

Taking a break on the bridleway between Anchor Lane and Barcombe.

4

Isfield and the River Ouse

The start of the walk at the Anchor Inn.

This is a **countryside walk featuring** the valley of the tranquil River Ouse in an area popular with walkers. Half of the walk is riverside and the return is across open country, woods and fields. Perfect for energetic dogs, with water to splash in, then following their nose through the woods.

Terrain
Mostly level footpaths and tracks with a few small inclines.

Where to park
Park by the Anchor Inn, Anchor Lane. Although close to Isfield, you cannot drive directly between the two. **Grid Ref**: TQ442159. **Map**: OS Explorer 122 Brighton and Hove.

East Sussex – A Dog Walker's Guide

How to get there

Heading north from Lewes on the A275 East Grinstead road, bear right at the Rainbow Inn about ½ a mile beyond the level crossing at Cooksbridge station and follow the signs for Barcombe. At Barcombe follow the road signposted for Spithurst, then turn first right into Boast Lane and then bear left by the post box. This becomes Anchor Lane, marked with the 'No through road' sign. Follow the lane to the far end. **Sat Nav**: BN8 5BS.

Refreshments

The Anchor Inn permits dogs at the bars but not close to the dining tables. There are lots of outside seats and tables in the gardens overlooking the river. There is a dog water bowl by the boating station. The pub is open all day every day and has a separate kiosk selling ice creams. ☎ 01273 400 414.

Dog factors

Distance: 2½ miles.
Road walking: A few hundred yards along a very quiet lane.
Livestock: The potential for sheep and encountering horse riders. There may be ground-nesting waterfowl depending on the time of year so please put dogs on leads where the notices ask you to.
Stiles: A few.
Nearest vets: Starnes & Blowey, Fairfield House, New Town, Uckfield TN22 5DG. ☎ 01825 764 268

The Walk

1 Cross the bridge over the river. Once over the bridge turn sharp left following the path with the river bank on your immediate left. Carry on alongside the river, passing underneath the iron bridge. Keep going along the path, at times it will be indistinct but the river will always be on your left, although not always immediately next to the path. After some time the path emerges onto a track next to a bridge over the river. Turn left and immediately cross the bridge.

2 Once over the bridge go through the gate facing you, now follow the path bearing left across the field. At the other side go through the gate following the waymarked arrow. Follow the path over the bridge as it snakes around a little, with the stream on your left. The path rises to a gate. Go through the gate and keep the hedge line on your right hand side where the paths diverge. Keep the hedgerow on your right and follow the path up through the trees. Carry on through the trees, and at the end cross the stile and turn sharp right. Follow the path round the corner of the field boundary.

❸ A few yards on at the waymarker post turn sharp left where the broad grassy track crosses the field.

You are now briefly following the course of an ancient Roman road. This is one of the lesser-known Roman Roads in the country and linked London to Lewes. Here it is just a path across a field, elsewhere its trace has disappeared completely whilst in other places (such as the dead straight road through the town of Edenbridge) its course still influences 21st-century daily life. Pottery fragments found near Barcombe have dated construction of the road to the 1st or 2nd centuries. Beneath your feet here Roman legions would have marched on a surface 15 feet wide made up of compacted flint, gravel and left-over slag from the Wealden iron smelting industry. There are still traces of slag from the road in the fields between here and Barcombe.

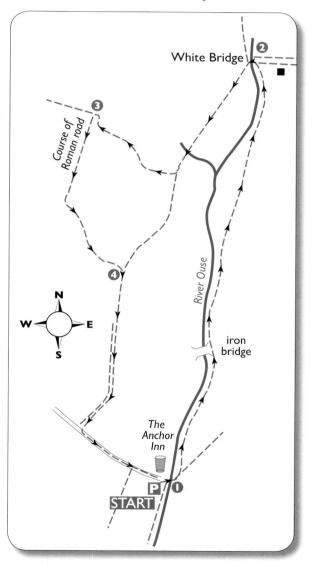

Springtime by the tranquil River Ouse, where the walk passes beneath the iron bridge.

You will soon have a small wood on your right hand side. When this ends bear left following the path and the field boundary, you have now left the course of the road. Where the field boundary bears left again, take the path in the right hand corner and then follow it round to the right.

4 Now carry on ahead, the field soon funnels into a track. Follow this to the very end and when it emerges onto a field keep the hedge line to your right. At the lane go through the gate and turn left. Follow the lane back to the starting point.

The Anchor Inn has an historic pedigree and is an ideal spot to relax after the walk. It dates back to 1790 and was a pub until 1895 when its licence was temporarily revoked after the landlord was found to be involved in smuggling. The pub has always been associated with the river. In Victorian times bargees would tie up here, their barges conveying cargo deep inland from the channel ports. Materials to build the local railway were brought up by water, but then it was the railway which killed off the barge traffic, which had ceased by the mid 1860s. Today leisure boating is available from the boat station at the side of the pub, from 10 am to 6 pm weather permitting – and dogs are allowed in the boats.

Seven Sisters Country Park and Cuckmere Haven

The iconic view of the Seven Sisters cliffs from Seaford Head.

This is probably one of the most iconic walks in the county, and also one of the simplest. It takes you down from the Seven Sisters Country Park to the sea at Cuckmere Haven, where your dog can have fun on the beach while you can admire one of the most famous views in the land. For this reason, the area is very popular with an estimated 350,000 visitors a year.

Terrain
Some road walking initially and then broad and wide paths with some open cliff top and beach.

Where to park
There is parking at the Seven Sisters Country Park Visitor Centre by the A259. There are car parks on both sides of the road. At the time of writing the parking fee was £3.50. Please don't park in the Cuckmere Inn's private car park. **Grid Ref**: TV519995. **Map**: OS Explorer 123 Eastbourne and Beachy Head.

How to get there
The Visitor Centre is on the main A259 Seaford to Eastbourne Road, a few miles east of Seaford and close to Exceat Bridge. **Sat Nav**: BN25 4AD.

Refreshments
The Cuckmere Inn (formerly the Golden Galleon) is at a marvellous location at point 2 on the walk. It is entirely dog friendly and is open all day. Outside, food is only served at the tables closest to the pub. It can get very busy indeed during the height of the summer. ☎ 01323 892 247. There are usually ice cream vans in the car parks.

Dog factors
Distance: 3 miles.
Road walking: Initially a short distance alongside the busy A259, unfortunately this is unavoidable.
Livestock: None.
Stiles: None.
Nearest vets: Beechwood Veterinary Surgery, 37 Stafford Road, Seaford, BN25 1UE. ☎ 01323 893 884

The Walk

· ·

❶ Start from the public car park at the **Seven Sisters Visitor Centre**, close to **Exceat Bridge**. There are car parks on both sides of the main A259 road. The

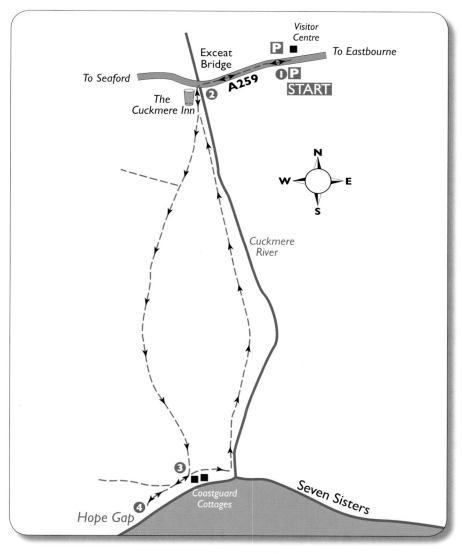

walk does start off with a short distance of walking alongside this busy road. From the car park on the Visitor Centre side of the road turn right. From the car park on the opposite side of the road, turn left. Keep on the slightly raised path on the left hand side of the road. Just before the bridge you will need to cross the road where the path finishes. Then outside the pub, you will need to re-cross the road into the pub car park.

2 Walk through the car park to the very end and go through the gate. Where you come to a crossroads of paths by an information board, go straight ahead through the gate. Follow the path right to the end. Where it opens out into a wide grassy area with the cottages in front of you, keep to the right hand fence line. Walk up the hill past the small war memorial.

You are now on the slopes of Seaford Head. As you look back down the hill you have one of the most iconic views in the entire country before you. The Seven Sisters are made from chalk that formed below the sea millions of years ago. The chalk is formed from skeletons and shells of microscopic plankton which sank to the bottom of the sea. The weight of the water above compressed them and over millions of years the sea bed rose then went down, leaving the compressed chalk high and dry. In more recent times the beach was a regular haunt for smugglers, hence the establishment of a permanent coastguard presence. The coastguard cottages are now holiday lets with only one permanently inhabited. Built as a coastguard station in the 1830s, the buildings were then well inland from the cliffs but erosion has brought them to the cliff edge. They are now protected by a large sea wall down on the beach. The scene has featured on TV and films countless times. In the film Atonement, *a postcard of the scene, an unobtainable idyll in the film, was a central element of the plot.*

3 There are plenty of benches dotted around so take a seat and drink in the view! In due course the walk will take you down onto the beach in front of you, but if you would like to visit a more secluded piece of seashore follow the footpath as it goes uphill immediately in front of the coast guard cottages and bear left following the cliff top. A short distance later you will see Hope Gap in front of you, with access to the beach down a flight of steps.

4 Then retrace your steps to point 3 close to the cottages. Walk back down the hill, this time keeping straight ahead down onto the beach. On the beach at low tide can be seen the remains of PLUTO, an acronym for *Pipe Line Under The Ocean*. This was laid along the bottom of the English Channel towards the end of the Second World War to pump fuel to France to support the allied army following the invasion of Europe after D Day in 1944. Continue to the far end where on the left you will see a raised footpath on the left hand

Spaniels on the beach at Cuckmere Haven. The famous coastguard cottages are well defended from the sea – for the moment.

side of the river. Follow this footpath all the way back to the pub car park at point 2.

Although it looks like a river, you are actually walking alongside a canal. In 1846 the Cuckmere River was diverted into this straight channel to drain the adjacent floodplain. The original river still meanders down the valley in a series of spectacular loops on the other side of the valley floor. In recent years the embankments of this Victorian channel have become increasingly unstable leading to a variety of controversial suggestions, including some to deliberately breach them. This would flood the adjacent wet grasslands and salt marshes and return the landscape to that of an estuary. It has been claimed that this would ultimately cause the destruction of the coastguard cottages which would then be eroded by the sea on both sides.

Once back at the Cuckmere Inn return along the road to the starting point.

Alfriston and the Cuckmere River

Alfriston's village green, known as The Tye, with the parish church and Clergy House.

This is a walk of real variety taking you up the high slopes of the downs; back down through one of the most famous villages in East Sussex and ending with a relaxing riverside meander. You are sure to have a happy and tired hound by the end of this walk!

Terrain
A small amount of road walking, wide paths and a steep gradient. The second half of the walk is entirely level.

Where to park
Alfriston village centre has two car parks. Dene car park off West Street is free but with a maximum stay of three hours. Across North Street the Willows car park is long stay but charges apply. **Grid Ref**: TQ 520032. **Map**: OS Explorer 123 Eastbourne and Beachy Head.

How to get there
From the main A27 Lewes – Eastbourne Road take the signposted turn at the Berwick roundabout. Both the car parks are in the village centre, Dene car park is a right turn, Willows left. These car parks become full very quickly in the day during the summer. **Sat Nav**: BN26 5UU

Refreshments
The Singing Kettle tea shop is in a prime position in the village square. There are outside tables and it is open from 10 am until 5 pm daily, although it may close earlier in winter if the weather is bad. ☎ 01323 870723.

The Star Inn is an Alfriston landmark and allows dogs inside. It is open all day. ☎ 01323 870495.

The village pub at Litlington at point 6 on the walk is the Plough and Harrow. Dogs are permitted inside and there is a small garden outside. It is open all day and serves food from 12-3 pm and 6 pm-9 pm on Mondays to Saturdays, and all day Sundays. ☎ 01323 870632.

Dog factors

Distance: 6 miles.
Road walking: About 1/3 mile initially and then later through the village centre.
Livestock: None.
Stiles: None.
Nearest vets: Beechwood Veterinary Surgery, 37 Stafford Road, Seaford BN25 1UE. ☎ 01323 893 884

The Walk

. . . .

1 From the **Dene car park** exit through the upper entrance. If you are parked in the **Willows car park**, cross the main road and walk back up through the Dene car park. Turn right along **West Street** (not sharp right into Sloe Lane). Carry on up the road for approximately 1/3 mile.

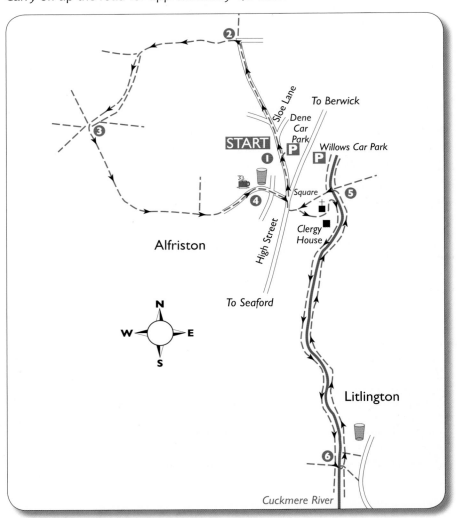

2 Where the road bends 90 degrees to the right, turn left onto the broad track. Keep ahead towards the hills. There are fine views inland on your right hand side with **Comp Barn** and **Berwick church spire** prominent. At the bottom of the hill take the middle of the three tracks that bear to the left into the woods. This will now climb steeply up the hillside.

3 Near the top there is a crossroads of paths. Turn sharp left. You now follow this track gently downhill all the way back to Alfriston. Where the path emerges onto the residential road keep going ahead.

4 At the crossroads at the bottom, cross the road and go straight ahead into **Star Lane**. You soon come out in the **High Street**.

The village square with its ancient market cross.

There has been a settlement at Alfriston since prehistoric times, the village takes its name from the Saxon Aelfrictun meaning the town of Aelfric. The ancient market cross is still central in the village square, which is surrounded on all sides by a wealth of historic buildings. The Star Inn was originally a religious hostel built in 1350 to accommodate monks travelling from Battle Abbey to Chichester. The Inn housed a so called 'sanctuary post' which provided instant protection to fugitives and smugglers.

Turn right, cross the road and turn immediately left down an alleyway signposted to the **Clergy House** and the church. This will bring you out on a wide grassy area known as the **Tye**.

The Tye is Alfriston's village green. In front of you is the 14th-century parish church of St Andrew, known because of its size as the 'Cathedral of the South Downs'. The wooden village sign on the Tye was carved by a previous rector. Next to it on the far right is the Clergy House, a rare thatched and timber framed 14th-century Wealden hall house. Although at one time it housed the parish priest and his housekeeper, it probably started life as a farm house. In 1896 it became the first ever property to be bought by the National Trust who paid £10 for it.

Bear right across the Tye, past the church until you are outside the Clergy House. Keep left between the church and the house and follow the path round the back of the church and right across the very small field.

5 Go through the gate and turn right. You will have another view of the Clergy House and the church on your right hand side. The river will be on your left. Keep following the path for a mile until you reach the first footbridge over the river. Turn left, cross the bridge and turn left again.

6 You are now walking back along the opposite bank. If you wish to visit **Litlington** village turn off the path to the right. (For the pub then turn left at the road). Keep going along the riverside path back to Alfriston. When you reach the next footbridge over the river go through the gate and turn left across it following the **South Downs Way** waymarker. Having crossed the bridge keep ahead along the alley and turn right at the **High Street**. In the village square bear left along **West Street** and the Dene car park will be on your right hand side, a few yards further on.

East Dean, Birling Gap and Belle Tout

A glorious summer's day at Birling Gap.

This walk is a classic day out and takes in some of the most famous landscapes of the South Downs National Park, in an area very popular with dog walkers. You will be walking along paths over the downs and on parts of the coast path along the cliff tops with plenty of things to see and do along the way, as well as lots of dogs to meet and greet.

East Sussex – A Dog Walker's Guide

Terrain
Wide grassy paths. A short distance along a very quiet country lane. There is plenty of hill climbing as you cross the contours of the Seven Sisters cliffs as they rise and fall.

Where to park
The Horsefield car park in the village of East Dean is free. There is a limited amount of on-street parking in the village. **Grid Ref**: TV557978. There is alternative parking at Birling Gap at point 3, but there is a charge and the car park gets very busy during summer weekends. **Map**: OS Explorer 123 Eastbourne and Beachy Head.

How to get there
From the main Eastbourne – Seaford A259 road at East Dean follow the signposts to the car park. Having turned off the main road the car park is a right hand turn off Gilberts Drive. **Sat Nav**: BN20 0DJ.

Refreshments
At the start and end of the walk, the Beehive café overlooks the village green at East Dean. Dogs are allowed inside and there are a couple of tables outside with a water bowl next to a convenient drain pipe for tying up! The café is open from 9.30 am to 4 pm Tuesday to Saturday, and from Easter until September also on Sunday from 10 am to 3 pm. The café also runs a delicatessen for picnics. ☎ 01323 423631.

At point 3 on the walk the National Trust has developed a visitor centre and tea room in what was the former Birling Gap Hotel. Anyone who knew the old hotel and has not been there for a while will notice a remarkable transformation! The tea room is open from 10 am to 5 pm. Dogs are allowed in an area inside, and outside there are tables overlooking the sea.

Dog factors

Distance: 5 miles.
Road walking: A very short distance in the village and a further section along a very quiet lane.
Livestock: Keep your eyes and ears open for grazing sheep on top of the downs.
Stiles: None.
Nearest vets: Chase Veterinary Centre, 89-91 Seaside, Eastbourne, BN22 7NL. ☎ 01323 639 331

East Dean, Birling Gap and Belle Tout

The Walk

1 From **Horsefield car park** take the exit at the furthest end where it rises towards the village green. When you are on the green with the war memorial facing you, turn left up to the road and turn right at the road. Walk up the road and follow it as it bears right. On the bend turn left up the driveway and through the gate at the end. Walk steadily uphill through the field, keeping the trees on your right.

2 At the top of the field turn left at the front of the gate but do not go through it. With the field boundary on your right walk to the gate at the end which is now facing you. Go through the gate and bear right across the corner of the field to the car park. Go through the gate and turn left through the car park. Take the gate at the end next to the cattle grid. Now follow the lane as it drops down to your right. Follow this to the very end. Where the lane ends carry on ahead along the footpath with the hedge line initially on your right. Keep going in the same direction until you reach the cliff tops and the coast path.

3 At the coast path turn left and follow the path all the way along the cliff top. After a mile, as it drops down towards Birling Gap, bear right down the short lane. At the bottom the **National Trust visitor centre** is next to the car park. There are steps down to the beach if your dog likes playing in the sea.

Birling Gap is a famous spot located mid way along the Seven Sisters range of cliffs in an area that suffers from constant coastal erosion. There only a few houses, the former hotel and a row of coastguard cottages built between 1800 and 1820. There were originally seven cottages, three have already succumbed to erosion, the last being demolished as recently as 2014 after being left just six inches from the cliff edge. The cliffs here can sometimes erode at the rate of 1 metre a year, leaving piles of fresh white chalk on the beach. The beach can be accessed by the large metal staircase, at low tide there are plenty of rock pools to explore.

4 Continue across the car park, the path starts again next to the phone box. Climb up to Belle Tout lighthouse on the next summit. Refreshments are sometimes available here.

Belle Tout lighthouse has been described as Britain's most famous inhabited lighthouse, it has featured in numerous film and TV series. It was opened in 1834 and used 30 oil lamps which required refilling at the rate of 2 gallons an hour. It wasn't a great success as fog would obscure the light on the cliff top whilst ships that had sailed too close couldn't see the light as it was blocked by the cliff edge.

East Sussex – A Dog Walker's Guide

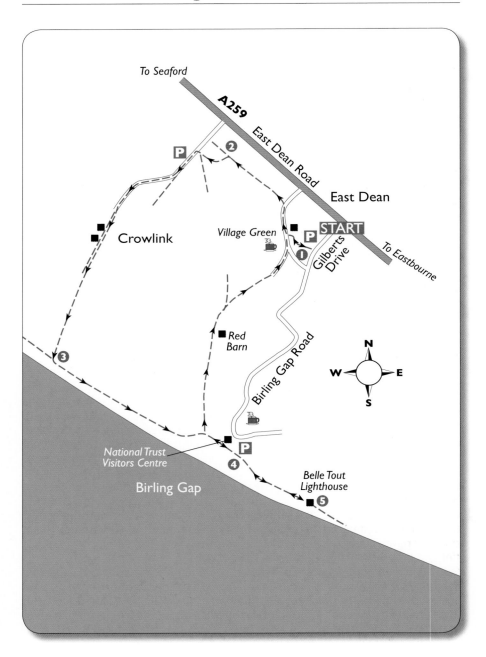

To Seaford

A259 East Dean Road

East Dean

To Eastbourne

Crowlink

Village Green

START

Gilberts Drive

Red Barn

Birling Gap Road

N
W — E
S

National Trust
Visitors Centre

Belle Tout
Lighthouse

Birling Gap

The picturesque village green at East Dean.

It was decommissioned in 1902 (and replaced by the famous Beachy Head light) and sold off in 1903 to start a second career. It passed through various owners until bought by the local council and restored in 1956. In the 1980s the BBC bought the lease to use the lighthouse as a location for a TV series, thereafter it has featured in films and music videos. In 1999, due to the threat of continued erosion, the whole 850 ton granite building was physically moved 56 feet away from the cliff face using hydraulic jacks, pushing the building along load-bearing beams. It was a pioneering operation then, but has since become more common in the construction industry.

5 Retrace your steps back down to **Birling Gap** and then back up the short lane between the houses. At the gate at the end this time turn right and follow the path as it climbs up the brow of **Went Hill**. At the top keep the red barn on your right. Bear right at the faint divergence of paths in the middle of the field. You are now heading for the right hand side of the field, although not the far corner. Follow the waymarker as the path drops through the woods back down towards East Dean. As the path emerges onto a lane keep going ahead, follow it round to the left and you will be back on the village green. Now retrace your steps back to the starting point.

8

Jevington

Jevington church nestling in the bottom of the valley.

This is an inland walk within the popular South Downs National Park area, but tucked away from the busier well known landmarks. It's a walk worth bearing in mind at the height of the tourist season when parking is at a premium at other popular venues close by. It takes you from a picturesque valley bottom village right up to the top of the chalk downs with fantastic views and back down into the valley again afterwards.

Dog factors
. . . .

Distance: 3½ miles.
Road walking: A very short distance in the village.
Livestock: Sheep a possibility, also horse riders.
Stiles: None.
Nearest vets: Chase Veterinary Centre, 89-91 Seaside, Eastbourne
BN22 7NL. ☎ 01323 639 331

Terrain
A very short distance on the road but otherwise tracks and paths.

Where to park
In Jevington village there is a free car park, but stay is limited to a maximum of 3 hours. **Grid Ref**: TQ562012. If this car park is full, try the car park at point 3 on the walk at the end of Butts Lane, **Grid Ref**: TQ580017. **Sat Nav**: BN20 9DP. **Map**: OS Explorer 123 Eastbourne and Beachy Head

How to get there
Jevington is on a minor road which links Friston on the A259 with Polegate on the A2270. From Brighton on the A27 and Uckfield on the A22 follow directions for Polegate and then take the Eastbourne Road (A2270) through the town, don't follow the directions for Eastbourne via the main A27/A22. The turn for Jevington is Wannock Road which is on the right at the traffic lights. Follow the lane through the downs until you reach Jevington, the car park is signposted and is on the right hand side in the middle of the village. **Sat Nav**: BN26 5QJ.

Refreshments
The Eight Bells is over 300 years old and is in the middle of the village. Dogs are allowed inside and there is a garden with country views outside. Dog bowls are also provided. Open Monday to Saturday from 11 am, Sunday from 12 noon. Hours may vary in winter. ☎ 01323 484442.

The Walk
. . . .

❶ Turn left out of the car park and then immediately right into **Eastbourne Lane**. Follow the track up the hill through the woods. After a while it will emerge onto the chalky slopes of the downs as it climbs **Bourne Hill**.

There are fine views back down towards the village. You will see the church tower through the trees. Parts of the church are Saxon and date from around the year 900. It is claimed the tower was a refuge from the Vikings who pillaged the area in revenge for the local population providing supplies to the army of King Alfred the Great. The area was rife for hiding smugglers' contraband which would be landed at secluded coves, such as Cuckmere Haven and Birling Gap, then taken up the quiet lanes and stored in cellars including that of the local rectory. More recently the village is also claimed to be the place where banoffee pie was created, there is even a blue plaque to mark the spot!

Follow the path to the very top. The landscape here is timeless; the chalk downs have changed little over the centuries. Down in the valley to your left are the remains of old field systems. Near the top keep going ahead at the first crossroads of paths.

❷ At the very top, at another crossroads of paths turn left, passing the triangulation point on your left. Keep going ahead. On your right are wide panoramic views over Willingdon and Eastbourne. On a clear day you can see across to Pevensey, Hastings and even the tip of Kent at Dungeness. Follow the track on the left hand side ahead towards the car park in the distance.

❸ At the car park turn left through the gate with the blue arrow waymarker, back down through Willingdon Bottom to Jevington. Just keep following the path

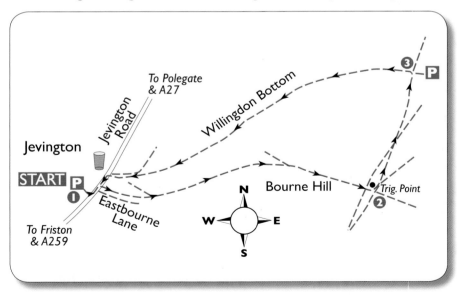

The view from the top of the downs between points 2 and 3.

down. Where the path bottoms out keep ahead with the fence on your right and go through the gate on the path, not the lower gate on your left. Where the path ends keep ahead along the short lane and turn left at the road at the end. The car park will soon be on your right hand side.

9

Eastbourne and Beachy Head

Overlooking the Beachy Head lighthouse from the top of the cliff top at point 3 of the walk.

Although short in distance, this will be good exercise for you and your dog as you are walking from sea level at Eastbourne up to the top of the cliffs. There's also the added bonus of a view of the iconic Beachy Head lighthouse. The South Downs Way is clearly signed and popular with dog walkers, so your hound should have plenty of opportunities to meet and greet, while you can stride along and admire the views.

Dog factors

. . . .

Distance: 2½ miles.
Road walking: None.
Livestock: None.
Stiles: None.
Nearest vets: Chase Veterinary Centre, 89-91 Seaside, Eastbourne
BN22 7NL. ☎ 01323 639 331

Terrain
Wide well trodden paths, but steep climbs!

Where to park
There is free on-street parking at the western end of the Eastbourne seafront road where it becomes King Edward's Parade and Dukes Drive. **Grid Ref**: TV 600971. **Map**: OS Explorer 123 Eastbourne and Beachy Head.

How to get there
Follow the signs to Eastbourne seafront and drive as far as you can in a westerly direction – that is towards the large hill. You can avoid driving through the town centre by taking the B2103 turn off the A259 on the west side of the town. Follow the signs for the seafront, the road will twist and turn downhill and as soon as it straightens out for the seafront stop at the first available place to park. **Sat Nav**: BN20 7XL.

Refreshments
There is a refreshment kiosk at the bottom of the hill at the start of the walk. It is open from 10 am to 5 pm during the summer months with outdoor seating and a water bowl for dogs. At point 2, set back on the cliff top road, the Beachy Head inn is dog friendly inside and out with a patio providing wide views to Belle Tout and Birling Gap. If eating, booking ahead is a good idea in summer but please advise the pub that you are bringing a dog as you need to be seated in the appropriate area. Open every day from midday, there is a water bowl outside the adjacent visitor centre. ☎ 01323 728060.

The Walk
. . . .

1 Park in **Dukes Drive** or **King Edward's Parade**, there are plenty of spaces and no charge at the time of writing. Walk up the road towards the bottom of the steep hill. Follow the **South Downs Way** waymarker and go straight up the steep hill and up the short flight of steps. Keep going and you will soon reach an isolated waymarker pole. Don't take the grassy way immediately to your left. Keep ahead for just a few yards and take the path that diverges now, slightly to the left.

2 You are still on the South Downs Way. Now you just keep going up and up all the way to the top! There are a variety of paths, it doesn't really matter which one you are on, but don't cross the road when you get to the top. Just keep to the left of the road towards the cliff top. Follow the concrete path as it now drops slightly down towards the viewing point and memorial. You will be sharing the walk with everyone who has either driven or got the tourist bus up the hill and who will not have been sharing your effort! Head for the viewing point and take in an iconic and well earned view.

Beachy Head itself is the furthest outcrop of the chalk headland and is the highest chalk cliff in Britain, rising 530 feet above the sea. The name is a corruption of the French name beau chef, meaning a beautiful headland. Using 3,660 tons of Cornish granite the famous lighthouse was built in 1902 and replaced the old one

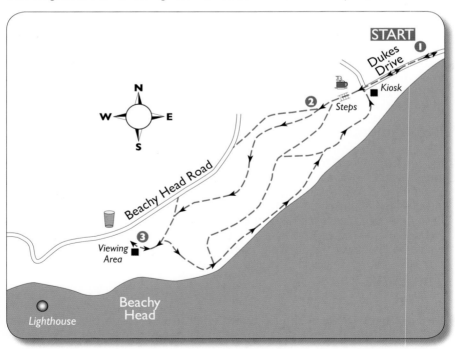

The sweeping view down from Beachy Head towards Eastbourne, showing the return path of the walk.

at Belle Tout. Construction took two years and required a cofferdam and cable way down from the cliff top. Until it was automated in 1983 it was manned by three lighthouse keepers, the light being visible up to 30 miles out to sea. In 2010, changes in navigation technology led to the visibility of the beam being reduced to 9 miles and the discontinuing of the use of its fog horn. It was also announced that there was no money available to keep painting its distinctive red and white stripes and the lighthouse would be left to weather to its natural granite grey. As a result, a sponsored 'Save our Stripes' campaign raised the £27,000 needed to keep the structure's distinctive colours.

3 Retrace your steps back and take the path where it drops sharply down the hillside on the right towards the sea. Just before you go down the hillside you will have a view of the path you are taking most of the way back. Follow it down to the bottom and bear left. You now keep going ahead with the sea on your right all the way back to Eastbourne. Where the path emerges at the refreshment kiosk turn right and you are back on **Dukes Drive**. If you want to extend the walk, take the turn where the road bears right and drops down to the seafront which you can follow for as long as you wish before doubling back.

Ashdown Forest

Far reaching views across the gorse-covered slopes of the Ashdown Forest at the start of the walk.

This walk takes in a tiny percentage of the 82 miles of tracks and paths that criss-cross this classic area. Just like the more famous New Forest, it is not a forest at all as much of it is open heathland. The area is famous for its broad expanses of open land picked out with clumps of yellow gorse. With its highest parts at over 700 feet above sea level, there are marvellous views in all directions. There are a lot of free-roaming animals grazing, as well as horse riding in the area – it is central to the ecology of the area. A board of conservation manages the forest and whilst dogs are welcome in the forest, the board emphasises the need for close control and the usual reasonable guidelines for being out with your animal.

Dog factors

Distance: 2 miles (4 miles for the extended version).
Road walking: None.
Livestock: Potential to encounter livestock grazing and horse riders at any point.
Stiles: None.
Nearest vets: Starnes & Blowey, Fairfield House, New Town, Uckfield TN22 5DG. ☎ 01825 764268

Terrain

The walk features wide paths and tracks which are often rutted and uneven. There is a long descent downhill and a corresponding climb on the return.

Where to park

There is a free car park at the Hollies, at the start of the walk. **Grid Ref**: TQ462286. The forest car parks can get fairly full and there is an alternative at Stonehill close to point 2 on the walk. There are also car parks on the opposite side of the road at both Hollies and Stonehill. **Map**: OS Explorer 135 Ashdown Forest.

How to get there

Take the A22 either south from East Grinstead or north from Eastbourne. Just north of Nutley take the turn signposted for Crowborough. The car parks are about 2 miles along this road on the right hand side. The car park signs are very small and are set low in the ground. If coming from the eastern side of the county, take the B2026 south through Hartfield. Follow the signs for Duddleswell but take the right hand turn signposted for Nutley just before you reach Duddleswell. The car park (Hollies will be first) will be on your left hand side, although the entrance is a bit obscure. The local roads all have a blanket 40 mph speed restriction due to the danger of grazing animals unexpectedly obstructing the road. **Sat Nav**: TN22 3JL.

Refreshments

There are no refreshment facilities adjacent to the walk, apart perhaps from the occasional marauding ice cream van in the car parks during the summer. The village of Nutley is a few miles away. Turn left out of either car park and then turn left at the end of the road onto the A22. There is a convenience store on the left hand side in the village which might be useful to stock up for a last minute picnic. Further on is the Nutley Arms, which features a café style operation and welcomes dogs inside. At the time of our most recent visit it was advertising opening hours from 9 am until 3 pm. It's probably best to phone ahead to confirm times when you visit – 01825 713322.

The Walk

. . . .

1 Starting from the **Hollies Car Park** locate the information board and looking out across the landscape turn right following the wide track that runs parallel (but at a little distance) from the road. Follow the track as it dips and turns through trees and then out into the open. After a little while you will pass a bench on your right hand side followed by a crossroads of tracks. At the crossroads there will be a wooded area to your left and an isolated tree to your right.

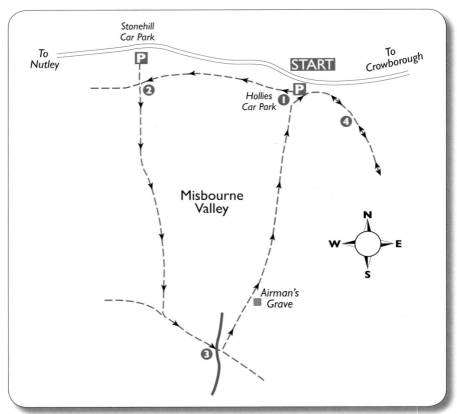

The evocative Airman's Grave.

2 Turn left and take the track through the trees and follow it all the way down the hill. At the bottom of the hill you will have a clump of mature trees ahead of you and another crossroads of tracks in front of them. Turn left and follow the track right down to the bottom of the hill where a small bridge crosses a stream.

3 Cross the bridge and turn sharp left up the hill. You will soon come across a small stone enclosure known as the **Airman's Grave**.

Despite appearances there is no actual grave here. The tiny garden inside the enclosure is a memorial to the six crewmembers of a British Wellington bomber from 142 Squadron which crashed here during the Second World War. The aircraft was part of a 100-strong bombing raid heading for Cologne in July 1941. A combination of appalling weather and engine malfunction saw the bomber ditch into the hillside with all on board losing their lives. One of the airmen who perished was 24-year-old Flight Sergeant Sutton. It was the young man's mother who had the enclosure and garden built in his memory. At her behest a memorial service is still conducted each year.

Carry on up the hill in the same direction. Where there is a divergence in the tracks keep going ahead. The wide path through the bracken here also serves as a fire break. At the top of the hill you will be back at the car park, however on the right hand side of the car park close to the exit there is a waymarked footpath sign pointing further up the hill. Take this path for a few hundred yards. It will bring you out on a broad plateau where you have one of the finest views in the county. On a clear day, you have a 180 degrees vista which takes in the 16 mile distant ridge of the South Downs, with the Misbourne Valley and Ashdown Forest as a foreground.

The Ashdown Forest was once a medieval hunting forest dating back to the Norman Conquest. By the year 1283 the forest had been enclosed by a 23-mile-long fence. Local people had the right to graze their livestock within the enclosure and this did much to suppress the growth of trees and scrub giving rise to the open views you see today. Once it was enclosed it is said that there were 1,500 deer, 2,500 cows and 2,700 pigs roaming around! There was still intensive grazing until the 1920s after which birch and oak trees started to invade the open land. In 1988 the bulk of the forest was bought from private ownership by the county council. Today the forest is managed by its own board of conservators, and at approximately 10 square miles is the largest open space in south east England. Grazing of sheep and cattle has been reintroduced and is encouraged to maintain the historic environment. It is recognised as a European Union Special Area for Conservation and is designated as one of the country's Areas of Outstanding Natural Beauty.

4 To end the walk just double back to the car park. Alternatively, if you wish to explore further you can continue along the path which drops back down the hillside and return when you wish. If you keep following the path (don't bear left) and turn right at the crossroads of paths near the bottom of the hill in the woods, you will return to the little bridge over the stream, and by returning back up the hill you can double the length of the walk.

Spa Valley Steam Railway and Groombridge

Full steam ahead on the heritage Spa Valley Railway at Eridge station.

This is a walk that is a little different from the others. It takes in woodland walks, together with the massive sandstone outcrops that are a rare geological feature of the landscape in this corner of the county. This walk is not circular, you can do part of it as a figure of eight, but much more interesting, and as a further attraction, is to let a steam train take you and your hound in one direction, and then walk back again.

Dog factors

Distance: 3 miles with the train; 4 miles without.
Road walking: Mostly along quiet country lanes.
Livestock: None.
Stiles: None.
Nearest vets: Culverden Veterinary Group, 4 Beechwood Parade, Walshes Road, Crowborough TN6 3RD. ☎ 01892 661 650

Terrain

A variety of footpaths, woodland tracks and quiet roads.

Where to park

If taking the train one way this walk should be done at weekends from March to October. Visit www.spavalleyrailway.co.uk or call 01892 537715 to confirm dates and times, especially which trains will be hauled by a steam locomotive. Dogs travel free on the heritage railway, provided they are kept on a short lead and are not allowed on the seats. At the time of writing, parking at Eridge station is £2.70 all day (£1.00 Sundays and Bank Holidays). **Grid Ref**: TQ 542345.

If not taking the train, park at the British Mountaineering Council's car park at Harrison's Rocks, off Eridge Road, south east of Groombridge village. There is a donation box in lieu of a specific parking charge. **Grid Ref**: TQ 533363. **Map**: OS Explorer 135 Ashdown Forest.

How to get there

If taking the train one way, Eridge station is situated on the A26 half way between Crowborough and Tunbridge Wells. It is signposted on the left hand side. Drive past the station entrance and bear left round to the car park. Alternatively, there are some parking places right next to the station entrance. Walk up the short flight of steps from the car park (or down the footbridge stairs from the station entrance if you have parked at the front). You are heading one stop on the train to Groombridge on the heritage Spa Valley Railway. Tickets for the train can be bought from the office on platform 2, not the main ticket office at road level. **Sat Nav**: TN3 9LE

If not taking the train, Groombridge village is on the B2110 south west of Tunbridge Wells. From the west take the A22 out of East Grinstead and then the B2110 at Forest Row. Once in Groombridge take the turn into Corseley Road at the mini roundabout and left into Station Road. Then bear right into Eridge Road, the entrance to the car park is not well marked and is on the right hand side. **Sat Nav**: TN3 9NJ.

Refreshments

Both of the pubs in Groombridge village – dating from 1585, the Crown Inn, on the village green (Tel 01892 864742) and the Junction Inn near the station (Tel 01892 864275) are both dog friendly. During the summer the Junction also operates a tea room in which dogs are permitted. There is a bakery and village shop in Groombridge whilst refreshments are also available from a kiosk at Groombridge station where dog water bowls are provided. At times refreshments are also available at Eridge station. Whilst on the move, most of the Spa Valley Railway's trains include an award-winning restored bar and buffet car offering real ales and cream teas.

The Walk

1 If starting at **Eridge**, take the train to **Groombridge**.

The Spa Valley Railway runs from Eridge to Tunbridge Wells along a section of line closed by British Rail in 1985. This was the last major piece of railway line that was closed in the entire UK. It was reopened in sections from 1996 until 2011. Everyone you see working on the railway is a volunteer. The steam and heritage diesel locomotives that pull the trains and the carriages that you ride in have all been painstakingly restored and maintained by the volunteer workforce. Eridge station was built in 1880 and was once the hub of a long forgotten network of rural railway lines across the county that ran from East Grinstead, Oxted and Tunbridge Wells down to Lewes, Brighton and Eastbourne. It was a bustling place where passengers changed trains, or the trains themselves would be divided and different parts would set off along different routes. It retains the atmosphere of a Victorian country junction with its immaculately restored buildings and even reflects the days when there was a separate waiting room for ladies!

2 Once you have arrived at Groombridge, take the exit at the far end of the platform and go straight along the station approach. Turn right at the end and then immediately left along **Springfield Road**. At the end turn left into

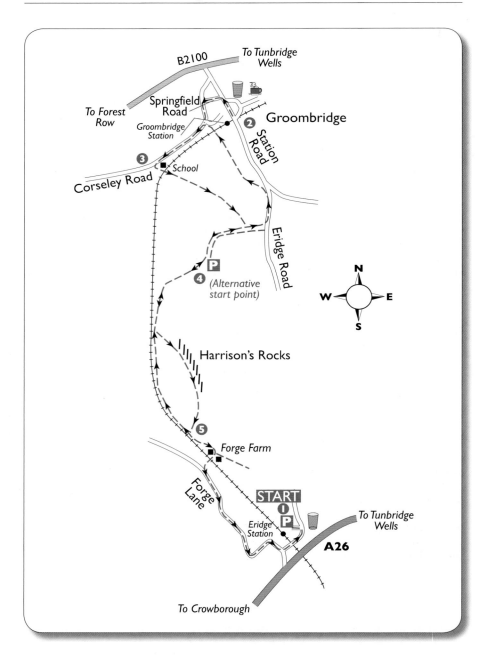

Corseley Road. Follow it round until you pass the school on your left hand side.

3 Take the footpath next to the school and cross the railway. At the end of this footpath turn right along the lane. Follow the footpath around the car park (or just cut diagonally through the car park). This will also be your start and finishing point if you have driven here.

4 At the south west corner of the car park continue along the path following the waymarked sign. Follow the path out of the woods and continue along it once it has veered left. Where the paths diverge take the left hand fork. You will now be passing along the base of the large sandstone outcrop known as **Harrison's Rocks**.

The rocks that you see today are millions of years old and were once the bed of a great glacier. For five million years sand and silt became tightly packed beneath ice forming hard sandstone rock. Warmer weather saw the ice melt away whilst later land erosion exposed the hard rock standing proud as it does today.

Carry on along the path until it comes to an end at a gate.

5 At the gate turn left along the path where the railway line will be to your right and below you. The path will drop down to **Forge Farm**, here take the right hand turn and cross the railway at the level crossing. Once over the crossing at the end of the track turn left. You now follow this twisting lane all the way back to **Eridge Station**.

Alternative walk without taking the train

This is essentially two joined circular routes and means that, looking at the map, you follow the sequence **4–5–4–3–4**.

Start at Harrison's Rocks car park (point 4). At point 5 turn right and take the lower path next to the railway back to the car park. Here carry on up the entrance track you drove down. Continue to the end and then turn left onto **Eridge Road**. At the end of this road bear left onto **Station Road** but take the access track almost immediately on your left after the white house. Keeping behind the houses, the track soon becomes a path. Keep going ahead. After the path crosses the railway, keep ahead along the driveway and at the road at the end turn left. Follow this road up the hill until you come to the school on the left hand side. You are now at point 3 on the main walk.

The Cuckoo Trail and Heathfield

Standing on the remains of the platform where Horam station once stood, on the Cuckoo Trail.

This is a walk of two contrasting halves, starting from the town of Heathfield and taking in the picturesque Cuckoo Trail to the village of Horam. The Cuckoo Trail follows the path of the former 'Cuckoo Lane' railway track and in muddy weather you could just do the first part of the walk as a 'there and back', as this level surfaced trail is always easy walking. The second half of this walk crosses fields and open countryside with plenty of opportunities for your dog to sniff around the hedgerows and burn off some energy.

Terrain

The first half of the walk along the Cuckoo Trail is flat and tarmacked as part of the national cycle way network. The return is cross country using lesser known footpaths which can be indistinct. We always wear our wellies for this walk after wet weather. There is a little road walking, mostly along a quiet country road in Horam and a short distance alongside a busier road in Heathfield towards the end of the walk.

Dog factors

Distance: 5 miles.

Road walking: Approximately 600 yards in Horam and a much shorter distance at the end of the walk.

Livestock: Be prepared for livestock in the fields you cross on the return and be ready to take appropriate precautions. We have encountered both sheep and horses.

Stiles: There are plenty. This walk involves lesser known footpaths where gates have not replaced stiles. At every stile we encountered we found ways that dogs could cross and all gates could be opened.

Nearest vets: Downland Veterinary Centre, 6 High Street, Horam TN21 0GJ. ☎ 01435 812152 (point 2 on the walk).

Where to park

There is a free car park at Newnham Way at the start of the walk. **Grid Ref**: TQ581213. If this car park is full there is a little on-street parking in Station Approach (turn left out of Newnham Way into Station Road and then left into Station Approach). There is further car parking in the town centre. **Map**: OS Explorer OL25 Eastbourne and Beachy Head.

How to get there

From the main A265 road through the town centre take the turn down Station Road. This will be on the right if coming from the west (A267) and on the left if coming from the east (A21). Newnham Way is then the second turn on the right. **Sat Nav**: TN21 8DA.

Refreshments

Wessons Café serves a whole variety of food and drink and is only 25 yards from point 2 on the trail at Horam. Just go up the steps opposite the name board and it is across the road facing you. It's open Monday to Friday from 7 am until 4 pm, weekends and Bank Holidays from 9 am until 4 pm. Dogs are welcome at the three large tables beneath the deep veranda at the front of the building. If the dog water bowl is empty, just fill it up from the green watering can!

The Walk

1 The walk starts from the car park adjacent to the start of the **Cuckoo Trail** in Heathfield.

Heathfield is a market town which stands on a hill within the High Weald Area of outstanding natural beauty. As long ago as 1316 it obtained a Royal Charter to hold a fair every April. According to legend an old lady would release the first cuckoo of spring from a basket, so giving rise to the fair's name – the Cuckoo Fair. When the railway came to Heathfield in 1880 local railwaymen called it the Cuckoo Line and the town re-sited away from the old village centre and developed around the new station. Five years before the coming of the railway there were only two buildings in what is now the High Street. In 1895 a bore hole looking for water for a hotel hit upon a supply of gas, it was the first find of a natural gas deposit in the country. For the next 70 years, various buildings in the town were lit from this local supply.

From the car park turn left along the Cuckoo Trail (also waymarked as National Cycle Trail No 21). All you do for the next two miles is keep going along the trail. Where the trail is crossed by **Ghyll Road** you may need to cross at the pedestrian lights and the continuation of the route is obvious a very short distance along **Treetops Way**.

A little further along look out for the old concrete railway milepost on the right hand side – this is your first hint of the heritage of the trail - which shows the distance as being 29 miles from Brighton. The Cuckoo Trail runs along the route of the old railway line from Tunbridge Wells to Eastbourne which closed to passengers in 1965 (by then it was only being used by 250 people each day) and for goods trains in 1968. The rails were taken up and the stations mostly demolished. In 1994 the route was tarmacked and converted into the trail which runs for 11 miles from Heathfield into the outskirts of Eastbourne.

Where the trail crosses **Tubwell Lane** keep going ahead over the narrow bridge, don't bear left down into the lane. Two miles from Heathfield you will pass underneath the curved arch of a bridge and the trail runs along a very short section of what was once the platform of Horam station. A couple of the distinctive old platform lamp posts and the concrete mounting for the station name board are remarkable survivors as they last saw a train 50 years ago. The actual name board is a modern replica. If you want to visit the village take the steps on the opposite side of the railway cutting up to the bridge and turn left at the top.

2 Walk past the sign and then immediately take a sharp left at the piece of modern sculpture and walk up to the road (this was part of the old station approach road). At the top turn right and then right again down **Vines Cross Road**. Keep going along this road for about 600 yards until there is a footpath on the left hand side. It is quite hidden and is next to the last house on the left hand side. If you have fields on your left and **Diamond Farm** on your right, you have missed it! It is opposite a small building with a small white turret in the roof on the other side of the road. The first part of the path is initially a driveway. Keep to this and not the parallel access road to the **Hidden Spring Vineyard**. Keep ahead, passing to the right of the five bar gate. At the next stile follow the direction of the waymarker bearing left and then immediately right up the broad vineyard access track. Keep ahead with the vineyard buildings on your right. Where the track ends go straight ahead over the stile. Carry on ahead with an orchard on your right until the next stile. Bear left and you will pass ponds on either side of you. Cross the stile which is now facing you, keep going in the same direction with the hedgerow next to you on the right.

3 Halfway along the field watch out for the gate in the hedgerow, and the ancient footpath signs deep in the greenery. The footpath now crosses from one side of the hedge to the other so either go through the gate or cross the stile and immediately turn sharp left with that hedge now on your left. At the end of the field cross the next stile, keeping to the right hand side of the field where there is another pond the other side of the fence. Very soon there is another stile in this fence. Cross this and the next one immediately opposite you. The right of way here is indistinct but head for the right hand side of the farm outbuildings. Go through the gate to the right of the buildings and again through the next one facing you. Now turn left keeping the tree line to your left down the field towards the house at the bottom.

4 Go through the gate at the left hand side of the house and keep going along the rough road. A short distance later the road dips down and bears sharp left. At the point that the road turns, two trackways turn off simultaneously to the right. Take the second one into **Sapperton Wood**. Keep to the right where the path diverges. Follow this path through the wood for about a third of a mile. In wet weather the path can get quite swampy but there is a drier alternative parallel on the left hand side. Make sure if you use this that you keep the original path in sight as this alternative path veers away to the left later on and will take you off the walk. At the end of the wood the path gets briefly quite narrow and twisted just before you emerge at a gate. There is now a 'crossroads' of five paths. Take the second on the left which will take you along a broad wooded track to the next stile. Cross over this and carry on along the next field keeping the field line to your left. At the end of the field there is another crossroads of paths.

5 Turn left and walk straight across the next small field, through the gap in the hedgerow opposite, over the tiny bridge and into the next field opposite. Keep the hedgerow to your right and after only a few yards watch out for the stile in the hedge. Go through the stile and turn sharp left following the waymarker, keeping the tree line now on your left hand side up the field. At the top of the field in the left hand corner there is yet another stile, cross it and keep the hedgerow to your left as you go along the next field. Ahead and to your right you can see distant views of Heathfield. Cross the stile at the end of the field. You will immediately see another stile opposite you, however do not cross it. Instead, bear right and follow the hedge line to your left hand side as it curves around. Keep on to the end of the field with the hedge to your left and again there is another stile at the end of the field. Cross this stile and go straight across the next field, however this field is home to horses so be aware. At the other side of the field there is yet another stile, once again cross it and again go straight across the next field. Both the path and the exit from this field are a little indistinct, head for the right hand side of the two largest trees on the horizon. Behind you and to your right are fine views of Old Heathfield and its church across the valley. Once you have gone through the gap in the hedge just follow the path up the hill, at the end cross the stile and bear left down onto the road. At the road turn right. Don't be tempted by the footpath through the trees on the right hand side of the road, you won't be able to easily drop down to road level when you need to. Instead cross the road and follow the pavement taking the first left down **Ghyll Road**. After the bend you will recognise the spot where the Cuckoo trail crossed the road at the pedestrian lights. Just before the lights, turn right back onto the **Cuckoo Trail** and retrace your steps back into Heathfield.

Pevensey Castle

The moat and 13th-century inner bailey walls of Pevensey Castle.

A **walk through one of the most well known** villages in Sussex, through the grounds of its famous castle and out across the adjacent marshes. This is a walk full of history across stunning Sussex countryside. The village of Pevensey is a delight to explore, with tile-hung cottages and a wonderful shingle seafront at Pevensey Bay. Dogs are allowed in the castle grounds, as long as they are kept on a lead. Open skies, marshes and a delightful village make this a walk you and your hound will both love.

Terrain

Varied on this walk with a little road walking in the village. This is a summer walk as after prolonged wet weather the footpaths across the marshes can get inundated with lying water and can get very boggy. The walk also passes through a working livestock farmyard so a lead is mandatory.

Where to park

There is a public car park on the east side of the castle. **Grid Ref**: TQ645564. **Map**: OS Explorer 124 Hastings and Bexhill.

Dog factors

Distance: 2 miles.
Road walking: A little bit in the village and the busy A27 to cross twice.
Livestock: This walk goes through livestock farmland and a working farm.
Stiles: No shortage!
Nearest vets: : Foreman and Hanna, 3 Mimram Road, Stone Cross, Pevensey, BN24 5DZ. ☎ 0871 978 3643

How to get there

The A259 from Hastings and the A27 from Eastbourne converge on a roundabout at the eastern side of Pevensey village. From the roundabout take the exit marked Pevensey and at the traffic lights go straight ahead. You will soon have the outer castle walls facing you. There is a small amount of on-street parking here but you will probably need to use the large car park which is on the left hand side as you drive up the road in front of the castle. Parking charges apply. **Sat Nav**: BN24 5LF.

Refreshments

The Royal Oak & Castle Inn is right next to both the car park and the castle. It is entirely dog friendly both inside and out and is open all day from 11 am. The beer garden at the back overlooks the village church whilst the tables at the front face the castle. Food is served Mondays – Thursdays 12-2 pm and 6 pm-8 pm, Friday 12-9 pm and Sundays 12-4 pm. ☎ 01323 762371. There has been a tea shop next to the castle by the car park for many years but on our last visit it was closed. Always famed for its cream teas we hope its loss is only temporary!

The Walk

1 From the car park turn left through the arch in the outer castle wall and pass through the gate into the grounds of the castle.

The first parts of Pevensey Castle were built by the Romans at a time when Pevensey was a raised hillock projecting out into a tidal lagoon, making it a strong natural defensive position. The Normans refortified it, building the inner bailey within the outer walls, so essentially building a castle within a castle as you can clearly see today. The current inner walls were rebuilt in the 13th and 14th centuries. It had fallen into disuse in Tudor times and Queen Elizabeth I gave an order that it be 'utterlye raysed', an order that was never carried out. Although sold to the state for preservation in 1925, the castle reassumed military significance during the Second World War. One of the concerns was that an invading force might capture it and use its position as a strategic stronghold. It was heavily defended with British, Canadian and American troops re-garrisoned here from 1940. Machine-gun posts were built into the walls, disguised as part of the original fabric.

With the wall of the inner bailey on your left, continue along the path and follow it to the opposite end of the outer castle walls. This was the site of the west gate of the original Roman fort. Turn sharp right into **Castle Lane** and follow it to the end.

❷ Cross the road and take the waymarked footpath through the gate opposite. After a few yards follow the waymarker pointing left. The path is indistinct. At the end of the field cross the footbridge. The next waymarker is a little misleading; the path does not diagonally cross the field. Bear slightly right

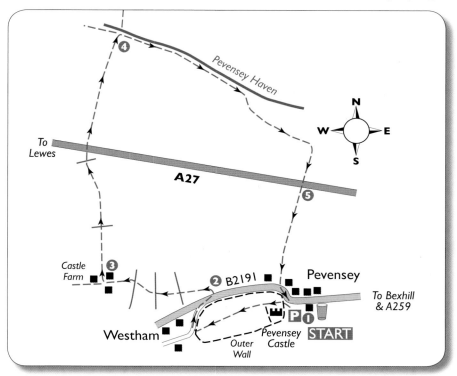

and cross the field. The exit from this field is waymarked and again you cross a footbridge. Immediately you pass through another gate. Follow the waymarker and there is yet another footbridge to cross on the other side of the field. Keep to the right hand hedge line, as the path gently rises to the farmyard. Cross the stile into the farmyard, following the waymarker. It is imperative you keep your dog under close control and on a lead as the path goes

Tile-hung buildings in Pevensey village, close to the market square at the start of the walk.

right through the middle of the farmyard within a few feet of open sided livestock sheds. In the middle of the farmyard turn right and follow the path as it gently drops down past more livestock sheds on the left.

❸ Follow the path into the next field. It is indistinct, but just follow the direction of the waymarker over the top of the brow of the low hill in front of you. On the other side of the field cross another bridge and follow the path over a stile and up to the road. Be careful as you have to cross the busy **A27 Pevensey bypass**. Continue over the other side. Now keep going in the same direction across the levels through a succession of fields and gates.

❹ You will finally reach a sturdy bridge over the **Pevensey Haven River**. Do not cross the bridge, instead turn sharp right and follow the river on your left hand side. You are now on the **1066 Country Walk**. After ½ mile the path bears to the right, away from the river, follow it through the gate. Continue along the path as it returns you to another crossing over the A27.

❺ Again cross the road and keep following the path. This will bring you to the castle walls and the village.

The village of Pevensey grew up around the castle and gained its own charter granted by King John in 1207. It became a town associated with the Cinque Ports but as their fortunes declined, so did that of Pevensey, which lost its borough status in 1886.

Turn left at the road, follow it round and you will be back at the start.

Herstmonceux Castle

Fine views of Herstmonceux Castle near the start of the walk.

A **walk through countryside and woodland** taking in a 15th-century castle and a 1950s astronomical observatory, whose fortunes have been very much linked in recent years. Although the name is decidedly French, the origin is Saxon, herste is a Saxon word for a clearing in the woods, and in the 12th century there was a marriage between the land-owning De Herst and De Monceux families. Dogs always loved walks in woodland and this stroll is sure to keep you both entertained.

Terrain

Footpaths and tracks with one very short stretch of road walking. One lengthy uphill gradient.

Where to park

There is a lay-by with plenty of spaces near the end of Church Road, south east of the village centre opposite the church. **Grid Ref**: TQ642104. **Map**: OS Explorer 124 Hastings and Bexhill.

East Sussex – A Dog Walker's Guide

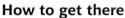

Dog factors

Distance: 2 miles.
Road walking: A very short distance with a verge.
Livestock: Potential for sheep and cattle in the fields.
Stiles: A few.
Nearest vets: Old Manor House Vet Surgery, Old Manor House, Market Street, Hailsham BN27 2AE. ☎ 01323 842 141

How to get there

Herstmonceux village is on the A271 between Battle and Hailsham. You need to take the turning into Chapel Row. This will be left just before the village if coming from Battle, and right just after the village if coming from the Hailsham direction. Carry on down the lane, after a while it will become Church Road. The parking place is on the left hand side a few yards before you reach the church. **Sat Nav**: BN27 1QJ.

Refreshments

There are no refreshment places on the walk, but you will have to pass either through or very close to the village when you drive in or out. In the village centre the Brewers Arms welcomes dogs in the snug bar. It advertises opening hours all day (although on our last visit it wasn't open at midday) ☎ 01323 831653. There is also a Mace convenience store and even a pet shop (Ruskos) for food and accessories.

The Walk

1 With the church on your right hand side continue a short distance down the lane. At the crossroads of paths with the farm buildings facing you, turn left, following the **'1066 Country Walk'** waymarker. Where the driveway bears right keep ahead through the gate. Carry on across the tarmacked area, cross the road and go through the gate facing you. Drop down through the woods and at the gate at the end keep going ahead. Here you get a good view of the castle.

The castle is one of the first large brick-built buildings in the whole country. Dating from 1441 it was never designed as a defensive castle, more as a self indulgent palace built for Sir Roger Fiennes, treasurer of the court of King Henry VI. By the 18th century the castle came into the ownership of a London lawyer and in 1777, following the whim of the day he had the entire interior demolished in order to reduce the castle to a fashionable picturesque ruin. It stayed that way until rescued in 1913 and a complete refurbishment and rebuild was completed in 1933. In 1993 it was purchased for Queen's University Ontario (Canada) and now houses an international study school.

2 In the middle of the field, next to the isolated tree, four footpaths cross each other. At the signpost turn sharp left. You are now heading to the far corner of the field at the right hand end of the wood that you have just emerged from. Follow the footpath to the left of the gate. Carry on over the access road and across the field facing you. Follow the path into the wood. Once you are inside the trees, ignore the immediate faint path that dog-legs to your right, but at the crossroads of paths a few yards further on bear right at the footpath sign post. Follow the blue and yellow bridle path waymarker with the green badge. Continue along this path until you emerge into the field. Carry on through the gate in the same direction, dropping down the hillside. A further path joins you from the left hand side. Almost immediately take the path on the right hand side just after the isolated tree, indicated by the waymarker with the green badge.

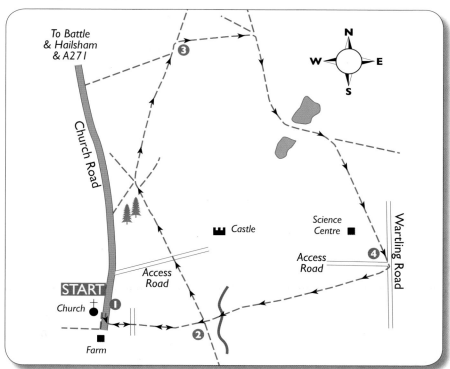

3 Continue across the field, pass through the gate on the other side and turn sharp right. Go through the next gate and continue ahead along the broad track. Follow this track as it gently turns down to the bottom of the valley. Then take the right hand divergence, with the path climbing back up through the wood. At the end of the wood cross the stile and continue along the path across the field in the same direction. Prominent on your right hand side are the domes of the science centre.

Herstmonceux is internationally known for its link with astronomy. The Royal Observatory, founded in Greenwich in 1675 needed to relocate by the mid 20th century due to increasing pollution and urbanisation in south London. The observatory took over the 15th century castle, initially moving in 1948. However, it wasn't until the 1950s that specialist buildings were constructed. What you see here are six large domes built to house the Equatorial Group of telescopes, three of which were linked by a building used to house photographic facilities and optical laboratories. The Fine Arts Commission suggested that the domes be clad in copper so that in due course they would blend in with the Sussex countryside. The facility still retained the name 'Royal Greenwich Observatory'. In 1967, a new state-of-the-art telescope was installed but eventually it was conceded that to utilise its full potential it needed to be on top of a mountain, not next to the woods and foggy marshes of East Sussex. Its relocation to the Canary Islands in 1979 heralded the decline of the observatory at Herstmonceux and as an astronomical observatory the facility closed in 1998.

4 At the end of the path, at the road, go through the gate and turn right alongside the road. Cross the access road for the castle and immediately afterwards take the path on the right, again waymarked **'1066 Country Walk'**. Cross the abandoned car park and follow the path into the woods. Carry on through the woods, about ½ mile later the path will bring you back to point 2 on the walk. Then retrace your steps back to the church.

The former observatory domes are an unexpected sight in the Sussex countryside. They are clad in weathered copper and now serve as an educational science centre.

Bewl Water

A beautiful day on Bewl Water with the oast houses that once belonged to Overy's Farm in the distance.

This is a walk around Bewl Water, an artificial reservoir built in the 1970s by flooding low lying valleys in the far corner of the county where it borders Kent. There is an eerie tranquillity about the lake; you will find some sounds carry for miles across the water. There's also plenty of space for your dog to burn off some energy, although they aren't allowed in the water itself.

East Sussex – A Dog Walker's Guide

Dog factors
. . . .

Distance: 2½ miles.
Road walking: About ½ a mile on one of the quietest lanes you will ever come across!
Livestock: No livestock, but you may encounter horse riders and waterfowl.
Stiles: None.
Nearest vets: Cinque Ports Vets, Cranbrook Road, Hawkhurst, Kent TN18 5EE. ☎ 01580 752 187

Terrain
Mostly wide tracks around the lake, one slightly steep climb up a footpath and some walking along a very quiet country lane. Dogs must be kept clear of anglers and wildlife and out of the water at all times. Don't let them drink the water if an algal bloom is present as it can cause fatal toxins when ingested.

Where to park
There is a large lay-by in Rosemary Lane on top of a small embankment at the eastern tip of the reservoir. **Grid Ref**: TQ 700318. **Map**: OS Explorer 136 High Weald.

How to get there
From the southbound A21 from Tonbridge, Rosemary Lane is a small right hand turn about a mile before the Flimwell crossroads. If travelling north from Hastings, it's a left hand turn a mile after Flimwell. Follow the lane until it opens out with the reservoir on your right and the parking spaces are on your right hand side. **Sat Nav**: TN5 7PT.

Refreshments
There are none on the walk but Ticehurst is the nearest village. From Rosemary Lane, head south and turn right into Berners Hill. Follow this to the end and turn right into Ticehurst High Street. The Bell Inn on the right hand side is entirely dog friendly and is open all day. ☎ 01580 200234. By the village green on the left hand side is a Londis convenience store if you'd prefer a picnic.

The Walk

. . . .

1 From the parking place where **Rosemary Lane** crosses the reservoir, head left as you face the water.

Bewl Water was first planned in 1946 but it was not built until the mid 1970s. Its purpose is to increase water supplies throughout Kent and Sussex. In 1973, the River Bewl was dammed and the valleys behind flooded to a maximum depth of 97 feet and now it is the largest body of inland water in the south east. The reservoir does not rely much on its own natural catchment; rather it is a storage area for water pumped in from elsewhere. Water is later released out into

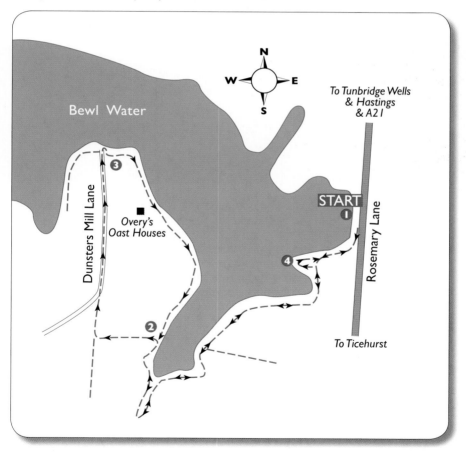

East Sussex – A Dog Walker's Guide

A rewarding sunset at the end of a dog walk. This is the view down the reservoir from the benches at point 4 on the walk.

the River Bewl beyond the main dam for abstraction further downstream. You won't see the large dam and overflow towers as this walk concentrates on the quieter east end of the reservoir, away from the sports and leisure facilities at the other side of the lake. If you want to visit these, the entrance is further north up the A21 and it is open from 9 am until dusk. There is a hefty car parking charge. There is a 13 mile 'Round Bewl Water Route', so if you fancy a more challenging walk just turn left when you get to the waterside at point 3 and keep going all the way around! We are assured it's all dog friendly but have never personally tried it.

Where the lane starts to rise away from the reservoir, go through the gate on the right hand side. Don't follow the footpath waymarker pointing in the opposite direction away from the water. You are now on the broad path that twists and turns with the inlets as it circumnavigates **Bewl Water**. You will be

72

taking the second footpath on the left hand side. It is shortly after where the path you are on turns sharply right as it crosses a stream.

2 Having taken the left hand turn, follow the path as it climbs up the hill. At the top turn right and continue along the driveway. Then turn right along the lane and carry on in the same direction. Follow it until you are back down almost at the water.

3 Next to the barrier at the end, just before the reservoir, you need to turn right following the bridleway marker. But just before you do, walk a few yards to where the lane now ends at the water's edge.

The road you have been walking along is Dunsters Mill Lane, but you have seen no mill. Dunsters Mill, together with its waterwheel, mill pond and Huntley's Farm next door were a few hundred yards ahead, but are now lost beneath the waters in front of you. The trees on the other side of the reservoir to the right are the remains of Mill Wood. Dunsters Mill Lane is one of many roads hereabouts that seem to serve little purpose and just disappear into the waters; a ghostly reminder of the valley's lost past. The actual Mill House was moved piece by piece to safety half a mile up the hill, although its waterwheel was left behind to be submerged by the lake.

With your back to the reservoir turn left at the bridleway marker, go up to the gate and carry on ahead. Continue back along the waterside path, passing point 2 on the way. Just before you get back to Rosemary Lane, where the path you are on cuts off a promontory, there is a grassy path to your left with the water on the left and pine trees to the right. Take this path down to the end of the promontory.

4 There are some benches at the end. This spot gives you some of the finest views down the whole length of the reservoir. On the left are the oast houses of Overy's Farm which you passed when you walked along the lane earlier. In the far distance is the main reservoir visitor centre. Return back to the main route, either along the path through the middle of the woods behind you, or carry on around the edge of the water, depending on the level of the reservoir. You will soon be back again on your outward route, then retrace your steps back to the starting point.

Bateman's

The fine Jacobean mansion at Bateman's which Kipling made his home.

'Day after day, the whole day through
Wherever my road inclined
Four-feet said 'I am coming with you!'
And trotted along behind.'

So wrote **Rudyard Kipling,** famed author of *The Jungle Book* and a myriad of other tales. The author lived at Bateman's for 34 years. Built in the 17th century and surrounded by the stunning Sussex countryside it was the place – despite his writing about India and the British Empire – that he regarded as his little bit of paradise. It is now owned by the National Trust who have recently allowed visitors with dogs into the grounds and gardens. The walk itself takes you round the Bateman's estate, through a landscape of fields, ponds and ancient woodland.

Terrain

Mostly footpaths through fields and woods. A little bit hilly in places and a small amount of road walking to start with.

Where to park

There is a National Trust car park which is free at the time of writing. **Grid Ref**: TQ671238. **Map**: OS Explorer 124 Hastings and Bexhill.

How to get there

Close to Burwash on the A265 (between Broad Oak and Etchingham). The turn for Bateman's is on the south side of the road a little to the west of Burwash village. Follow the lane down the hill for ½ mile and the car park is on the right hand side before the house. It closes at 5.30 pm, or dusk if earlier. There are very limited opportunities for parking in the surrounding lanes. **Sat Nav**: TN19 7DS.

Refreshments

There is a tea shop at Bateman's but you will have to pay the entrance fee for the gardens. Dogs are welcome at the tables outside – water bowls available. The Rose and Crown in Burwash village is a Harveys pub dating back to Tudor times with its own well. It allows dogs in the bar area and has a pleasant outside seating area. It is situated on Ham Lane, which is a left hand turn off the main road through the village if you are approaching from the Bateman's direction. Food is available lunchtimes and evenings but it is best to phone in advance to confirm times: ☎ 01435 882600.

Dog factors

Distance: 2½ miles.
Road walking: Initial few hundred yards along a very quiet lane.
Livestock: Horses stabled in a field at point 4.
Stiles: Plenty, but all dog negotiable one way or another.
Nearest vets: Heathfield Vets, Chimneys, Hailsham Road, Heathfield TN21 8AD. ☎ 01435 864 422

The Walk

1 Walk back down the car park approach road and turn right into the lane at the end. You will be passing the main house behind its high hedges on your right hand side. There is a sneaky view of the house through a gate in the hedge. Keep right with the hedge on your right hand side and follow the lane until you reach some cottages and the back of the mill on your right. At **Park Mill Cottage**, turn right off the lane following the waymarked sign. You will see the **Mill Pond** straight ahead of you.

The earliest mention of the mill and pond dates from the 1700s, but Kipling claimed it dated from 1196. There is the original watermill and a turbine which was one of the first ever domestic water turbine electricity generators. You can see the turbine if you look down on your right hand side just after the mill building. The pond itself is home to ducks and dragonflies.

Skirt the pond around the right hand side following it almost three quarters of the way round, and then take the path with the watercourse on the left hand side. Keep going over the tiny weir at the end and go through the gate.

2 Soon there is a right hand path (waymarked) which crosses the river on your right hand side, take this turn, cross the river and cross the field on the other side. When you get to the other side follow the path to the right over the stream and at the stile turn sharp left, following the red National Trust waymarker. Keep the field line to your left and at the gate and stile keep going ahead in the same direction up the broad track. Carry on up the track passing the abandoned barn.

3 Where the track emerges onto the lane, keep going ahead a short distance and then turn left, again following the red waymarker. Cross the next field bearing slightly right. Carry on into the wood and keep going past the ponds on either side. At the end of the wood, cross the stile and cross the next field. At the end, pass through the gate and keep to the right hand boundary of the field.

4 After crossing the next stile you need to turn sharp left. This is not waymarked but the footpath now drops down the hill keeping to the left hand hedgerow.

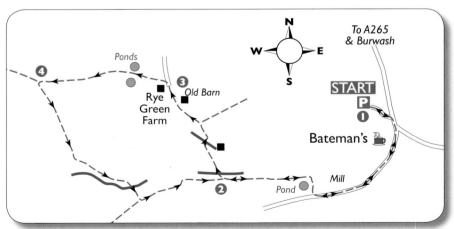

Follow it down to the bottom where you will see a gate leading into the woods. Go through the gate and follow the path as it twists through the woods. Carry on through the gate at the end into the field keeping the river to your right. Soon the path turns right out of the field and over a bridge crossing the river. Cross the bridge and turn left, again following the red waymarker. Go

Owned by the National Trust, the beautiful gardens at Bateman's now welcome dogs.

through the gate at the other end of the field with the river now on your left. About half way across the field the path now unexpectedly turns left over another bridge. Take this and turn right when you are in the next field. Again, follow the path across the field and into the trees. You will soon be back at point 2 where you retrace your steps back to the start.

You may want to visit the house and gardens either before or after the walk. There is plenty to see and the National Trust has extended the access available to dogs. Dogs are not allowed inside the house, but if there are two of you there is enough to see outside to take it in turns looking after the dog while the other person looks around the house. Dogs (under close supervision and on short leads only) are now welcome in most parts of the gardens if kept on defined paths. They are not allowed in the walled Mulberry Garden or on the manicured lawns. There is the usual reasonable request about clearing up. Inside the Jacobean manor house, built in 1634, the rooms are still as furnished by the Kiplings, who created interiors to complement the building's history. Much is left as it was at the height of the author's literary fame, including his book-lined study, his writing tools, paperweight and even his pipe. It is said that the family instantly fell in love with the place when they first saw it whilst house hunting in 1900. Outside there is the pond, wild garden, river, watermill and even the pets' graveyard, the last resting place for some of the family's much loved dogs. Currently the gardens are open daily (except 24th and 25th December) from 11 am to 4 pm, November to February, and 10 am to 5.30 pm March to October.

Hastings Country Park and Fairlight Glen

Dropping down out of Ecclesbourne Glen towards the sea, with Hastings harbour in the distance.

This is an undulating walk up and down the glens of the Hastings Country Park including some fine cliff top sea views and (depending on the state of the footpath at the time), a chance to visit one of the most little known, and dog friendly, beaches for miles around. The walk visits Fairlight Glen which was a popular attraction in Victorian times and the twisting paths make for a rewarding dog walk today.

Terrain

This walk is entirely along footpaths through the country park. It can be hilly in places with some steep inclines.

Where to park

There is a public car park for the country park off Barley Lane. At the time of writing the charge was only £2 for an all day stay. **Grid Ref**: TQ 838105. **Map**: OS Explorer 124 Hastings and Bexhill.

How to get there

From Hastings seafront take the A259 in the direction of Rye. Opposite the church turn right and then bear left into Harold Road. Then turn right into Barley Lane. The car park is on the right hand side (the entrance is a bit hidden) ¾ mile further on just before the holiday camp. **Sat Nav**: TN35 5NT.

Refreshments

None on this walk but there is no shortage of benches dotted around with fine views to stop and picnic at. Coastguard Tea Rooms are entirely dog friendly and are a couple of miles away. From the car park turn right. At the far end of Barley Lane turn left, then next right into Fairlight Road, then second right into Coastguard Lane. **Sat Nav**: TN35 4AB. Open Tuesday to Sunday, April to October, until 6 pm, November to March until 5 pm. ☎ 01424 814131. Hastings seafront is only a couple of miles away for take away fish and chips.

Dog factors

Distance: 4½ miles.
Road walking: None.
Livestock: None.
Stiles: None.
Nearest vets: Coopers Vets, 309 The Ridge, Hastings TN34 2RA.
☎ 01424 751 595

The Walk

1 From the car park in **Barley Lane** take the footpath through the gate in the left hand corner. As you start to drop down the hillside bear right where the

East Sussex – A Dog Walker's Guide

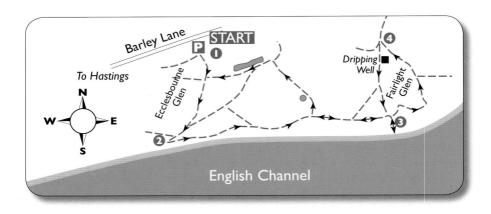

paths diverge. At the bottom of the valley where there is a crossroads of paths, carry on straight ahead.

The Hastings Country Park comprises nearly 700 acres of ancient woodland, grass and heathland together with dramatic coastline and cliffs stretching for five miles around Fairlight and Hastings. Most of the park has been designated a Special Area of Conservation and a Site of Special Scientific Interest. Ecclesbourne Glen, which you are walking through now, has been declared of national importance as home to sensitive ferns and mosses. In the spring the glen has an amazing display of bluebells and wood anemones. The Glen was the landing place and entrance to an Iron Age hill fort.

Carry on slightly uphill and bear right when you come to the open field in front of you. Now follow the wide path as it drops gently towards the sea. Keep going to the very end of the path where there is a bench and a view point looking out towards Hastings harbour.

Hastings has an ancient history. Around the time of the Norman Conquest it was a thriving fishing and trading centre. Until the 16th century it was a powerful maritime centre, and one of the famous Cinque Ports. You can see from here the remains of the harbour arms. In 1896, a grand scheme to create a safe haven was started, Hastings' previous harbour having been destroyed in the great storm of 1287. Work stopped when construction hit a mud-filled section of the seabed. After this setback the money ran out to complete the work. The uncompleted harbour arms were left in place but were partly blown up in the Second World War to prevent their use as a landing point for any German invasion.

❷ From the viewing point, turn around and with your back to the harbour take the path along the cliff top with the sea to your right as it gently climbs uphill. Keep to this path, always bearing right where other paths either join or diverge. A mile from the viewing point you will start a steep descent into **Fairlight Glen**. Keeping right, stay on the path until you have dropped right to the bottom of the glen where the path crosses a small stream.

3 At this point you may have the chance to walk right down onto the beach. The path is a right hand turn just past the bridge which you follow downhill, initially with the stream on your right hand side. However, this very much depends on the state of repair of the footpath given the frequency of cliff erosion. If erosion is an issue, there are usually signs indicating this and you must heed any warnings or advice. The path to the beach can be a bit precarious in places and at the best of times you should use your own judgement as to the safety of proceeding. If you are able to make it down, you will be rewarded with a beach scattered with rock pools and with a wide area of sand at low tide. As you are far away from the nearest car park this beach is one of the quietest for miles around and is a great place to throw a ball for your dog. Unlike most resort beaches, dog access is unrestricted year round. To return to the walk, retrace your steps to point 3. Now carry on in the same direction as if you had not turned off for the beach. Continue along the path that climbs up the opposite side of the glen to that which you came down along. As it climbs out of the woods keep following it around. After it turns inland keep ahead with the glen falling away on your left. At the end of the path turn left, do not go through the gate to the right.

4 You are now at the top of **Fairlight Glen**. Having turned left within a few yards you will see the Country Park marker post number 15. Keep to the left of the post and take the path as it drops back down into the glen. A few yards further on another path on the left drops down to the **Dripping Well**. It's only a very short distance down if you want to take a look. The 'well' is a small waterfall which drops down a rock face into a pool set in the glen. In Victorian times it was considered a great attraction. Returning to the walk, now follow the path right down to the bottom. You will have returned to point 3. Turn right and retrace your steps back up the side of the glen. Just before you come out of the woods at the top you will see marker post number 12. Turn right here and follow the path as it gently leads uphill until it comes out at the fields. On your left you will have long views back towards Hastings. Where the path drops back into the woods you will see marker post number 9. Although this directs you to turn right for Barley Lane, instead turn left here as this will cut out road walking later on. Having turned left follow this path all the way downhill, passing the reservoir on your right hand side. At the crossroads of paths, you will be back to marker post number 7. Here turn right and retrace your steps back to the car park.

18

Bodiam Castle and the River Rother

Bodiam Castle, said to be one of the finest castles in the whole country. Although it looks picturesque from the outside, inside it is sadly just a ruin.

A **walk featuring one of the most iconic sights** in East Sussex – the fairytale Bodiam Castle. This is one of the shortest walks in the book but there is plenty to occupy everyone at Bodiam itself. Then you and your four-legged friend can have a quick sniff round and head for a stroll in the countryside. It's a location where there is an amazing amount of history all within a small area, and this walk takes it all in.

Terrain
A variety of broad paths around the castle, a little bit of road walking with pavement or verge and some less used footpaths.

Where to park

Use the National Trust car park at the castle, although it is best to get there early as on busy days it can get full. At the time of writing the fee was £3 for non National Trust members. Parking at Bodiam is at a premium and there are parking restrictions in the adjacent lanes either all year round or from April until September, depending on proximity to the castle. There is no parking available at the station. **Grid Ref**: TQ 783254. **Map**: OS Explorer 136 High Weald.

How to get there

From the A21 south of Hurst Green follow the signposted left hand turn for Silver Hill and Bodiam. Bodiam is three miles on. When you drop down into the village the car park is on the left hand side of the road immediately opposite the Castle Inn. **Sat Nav**: TN32 5UD.

Refreshments

There is a National Trust tea shop in the car park and dogs are welcome at the outside tables. It can get very busy at lunchtimes, the outside seats can get taken quickly and service can be a bit slow. As you won't be able to sit inside with your dog it may be best to avoid peak times. The Castle Inn, right opposite the entrance, is a Shepherd Neame house and features a good selection of their Kentish Ales. It is open all day every day and dogs are allowed in the bar area. ☎ 01580 830330.

Dog factors

Distance: 1½ miles.
Road walking: A little road walking at the start of the walk, but there are either pavements or a grassy verge.
Livestock: The fields between points 2 and 3 are used to stable horses.
Stiles: Several, and one, in point 3, is not suitable for a large dog that you cannot help over.
Nearest vets: Cinque Ports Vets, Cranbrook Road, Cranbrook, Hawkhurst TN18 5EE. ☎ 01580 752 187

The Walk

1 From the car park there are two public footpaths which take you past the castle. They are both yellow waymarked and access is through gates on the opposite side of the car park across from the tea room. One of these is confusingly marked 'No access to the castle'. You can get some good views from these rights of way but if you wish to explore the grounds in detail there is now a ticket which should be bought. The ticket office is at the far end of the car park. Head up the path to the castle and take some time at the top to take in the spectacular scene.

This is one of the landmarks of the county. It was built in 1385-1388 by Sir Edward Dalyngrigge, a knight in the court of King Richard III. The king gave him orders to 'strengthen and crenellate' his manor house. Sir Edward then went a bit overboard as he abandoned his existing home and built himself the castle. Who knows whether he built the castle out of civic duty to defend the countryside from potential French invasion, or he was simply showing off, although in fairness the

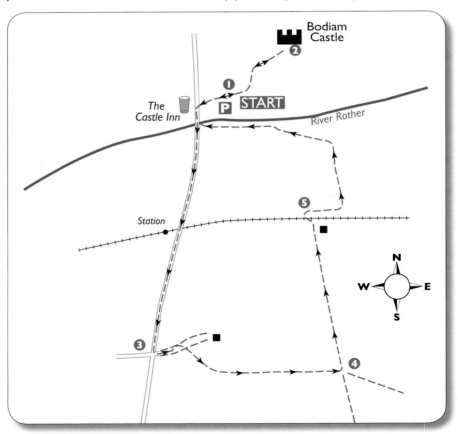

location he chose was a logical one. You would not believe it today but in the 14th century the tiny River Rother (which you may not have even noticed by the car park) was still navigable by sea-going ships all the way from the English Channel. In the event there was never a shot fired in anger at foreign invaders, however there was a siege in the 15th century. Orders were given for the interior of the castle to be destroyed in the Civil War and its exterior gently decayed until 1829, when John Fuller bought it to prevent its demolition. In 1916 the Marquess Curzon, Viceroy of India, bought the castle, restored the exterior and left it to the National Trust in 1925.

❷ Taking the full circuit around the moat will take you off the public paths. Return back down the hill and exit the car park turning left onto the road. Cross the river bridge, the pavement will be on the left and then the right hand side of the road. Once over the level crossing, the heritage Kent and East Sussex Railway's **Bodiam station** is on your right.

Hop growing was the major agricultural industry around Bodiam right up until the 1960s. Behind the station there is a small exhibition showing what life was like for those who harvested the crop. The bines were grown up poles covering acre upon acre of the local landscape. Around Bodiam much of the hop gardens (a field of hops is always known as a garden irrespective of size) were given over to the Guinness Brewery which then brewed in west London. Families from impoverished areas of south and east London would travel down for a working 'holiday' each harvesting season to strip the hops off the bines to be sent for drying in the oast houses, with their distinctive cowls. They would endure conditions on the farms that could be described as primitive in the extreme. A local clergyman described the workforce, saying 'Nothing more squalid can be imagined – they often appear to be one seething mass of rags and tatters'.

❸ Carry on up the grass verge on the right hand side of the road up the hill. Take the next left (opposite the broad entrance to **Quarry Farm**). The access track here will soon bend to the left. On the bend take the footpath on the right. This is probably the most hidden footpath we have ever come across. Even following a map we missed it twice – if you go beyond the bend and have an oast house facing you, you've gone too far. Follow the path over the stile, over the field, over the next stile and over the next field. The next stile may be problematic; the only way to cross on our visit was to carry our animal over it. Fortunately, it is fairly low. Carry on down the next field keeping the hedgerow on your left hand side. At the bottom pass through the gate.

❹ Now turn left, it's not waymarked but the path keeps to the left hand side of the field. Head for left of the abandoned agricultural building at the far end. The path will be obvious where it crosses the river. Follow the path round

The walk takes you over old Bodiam Bridge, built in 1797. Until 1385, the River Rother was so wide here that it was crossed by a ferry. It's hard to believe that ships taking cargo to France once navigated the river this far inland.

when it gets to the railway line. The path across the railway is marked by stiles either side and warning signs, but surprisingly there is no actual boarded crossing over the tracks, so be very careful to keep an eye and ear out for trains and take care not to trip on the rails.

5 Having crossed the second stile, turn right and follow the path around the outside of the large field in front of you. Keep to the footpath on the raised edge of the field; don't be tempted to cut across the marshy middle! The castle will be clearly in view so that you can orientate yourself around the field and back out onto the road close to the car park. When you return to the bridge take a look down at the **River Rother**.

It's hard to imagine that this was once the sight of a busy industrial wharf where sea-going ships tied up and freight was transhipped for over 2,000 years. It started off with exporting the products of the ancient iron industry which the Romans shipped away, down the Rother and off to their empire. When Sir Edward built the castle he built a wharf here to bring goods in and out, and even up until the 1950s barges came up river from Rye to deliver coal to the village. Between April and the beginning of October it's now possible to take a rowing boat out or take a gentle 45 minute cruise down river to Newenden. Dogs go free. ☎ 01797 253838.

Winchelsea and the Royal Military Canal

The remains of St Thomas's church are central to the historic town. The length of the original building can be judged by the width of the ruined remains of the nave.

This is a walk packed with variety and things to see. It takes in the historic centre of medieval Winchelsea, quiet lanes, footpaths and a canalside walk. You could choose to start this walk in the same place as Walk 20, visiting Rye and Camber, and if you combine the two you can give yourself a 9 mile walk, an option if you have a working dog who needs a lot of exercise. However, in this area there is just so much to see and take in, so we have divided the area into two separate walks.

Terrain

A little bit of road walking, a very short distance initially in the historic town centre where caution should be exercised. There is about ½ mile along a secluded lane which sees little traffic. Otherwise along paths and tracks, there are a few gradients to climb.

Where to park

There is on-street parking in Winchelsea. There are some spaces at the very start of the walk opposite the New Inn, if you are parking elsewhere in the town please do so considerately. **Grid ref**: TQ 904173. **Maps**: OS Explorer 124 Hastings and Bexhill, or OS Explorer 125 Romney Marsh.

Dog factors

Distance: 4 miles.
Road walking: : A little road walking, but mostly along quiet lanes.
Livestock: Sheep can be encountered at various places.
Stiles: One stile at the end of point 2 that you may need to lift your dog over. If you think this will be a problem, it would be better to return from the bird hide the way you came and resume the walk on the return to the New Gate at point 4.
Nearest vets: Cinque Ports Vets, Rye Veterinary Surgery, Cinque Ports Square, Rye TN31 7AN. ☎ 01797 222265

How to get there

The old town is just off the main A259 Hastings to Rye road. The main road skirts the historic centre but plenty of turns off the main road will give you access. Once in the old town the church is an unmissable landmark. **Sat Nav**: TN36 4EN.

Refreshments

The New Inn at the start and end of the walk is dog friendly inside and has a beer garden as well. It is open from 11.30 am on Mondays to Saturdays and 12 noon on Sundays. Kitchen service times are 12 noon to 2.30pm and 6pm to 9pm Mondays to Saturdays and on Sundays from 12 noon to 3pm and 6pm to 9pm. ☎ 01797 226252.

The Walk

1 Start the walk in the middle of the town in **German Street** with the entrance to the churchyard opposite the **New Inn**. With the church on your left hand side walk down German Street.

Winchelsea was founded in 1281 by King Edward I and was built as a new town to replace a predecessor destroyed by some of the greatest storms in the history of England. It was laid out on a grid pattern; some claim that the Winchelsea grid was the basis for laying out the city of New York! It soon became one of the most important ports in the south of England. The town has one of the greatest concentrations of medieval cellars in the country – testament to the prosperity of the 14th-century wine trade. However, its prosperity began to fail when its harbour silted up and the town was subject to continuing French attack. Having lost its trade and importance by the 1500s the town drifted into decay and slumber. Today the town is brimful of reminders of its past, its streets crammed full of character and ancient houses, the court hall next to the start of the walk being the oldest. On your left the most prominent building is St Thomas's church. It was originally the size of a cathedral with a landmark tower and spire, the nave stretching back across the churchyard right up to the road you are walking along. Around the end of the 16th century the main part of the church was demolished, possibly to reduce the cost of maintenance which was a burden on the town's declining fortune. This left only the former chancel which became the totality of the remaining church.

The road will change its name to **Monks Walk**, keep walking ahead out of the town. Where the main road bears right, keep ahead along the tree-lined lane. After ½ mile you will pass through the 14th-century New Gate. Shortly after

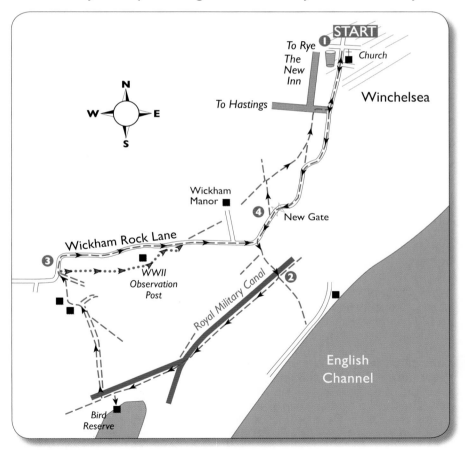

you have passed through the gate the lane bears right. At this corner take the footpath on the left that drops down onto the levels, follow it around the tree line on your right and immediately turn left following it across the field. Cross the bridge over the canal and once on the other side, turn sharp right following the canalside path.

This is the Royal Military Canal. It was built between 1804 and 1809 as a defence against feared Napoleonic invasion. It runs right behind Romney Marsh and Pett Level from Hythe in Kent to Cliffend a few miles away to the west. It was built using pick, shovel and wheelbarrow with the excavated soil used to form the defending raised bank behind it. Notice that it kinks every so often, this was to allow defenders a clear sight of fire along the length of it. By the time it was finished, the threat of invasion had receded and it has remained an expensive white elephant ever after.

2 Now keep ahead with the canal on your right hand side. At the first bridge you come to, turn right and re-cross the canal. Keep ahead over another bridge but do not turn right over the watercourse on your right hand side. Keep going ahead. On your left hand side there is an entrance to a bird hide. This is part of the **Pannel Valley Nature Reserve** and the hide overlooks a flooded area of the marsh teeming with bird life. Dogs are allowed inside provided they are quiet and on a lead. Please close the observation hatches before you leave. Resuming the walk, take the next footbridge over the watercourse on the right. Once over the bridge bear right and follow the track as it turns left heading up towards the hill. Keep ahead uphill through the gate. Near the top where the track bears right take the waymarked footpath on the left. Follow it through the trees, around the side of some buildings and up some steps. You will now encounter a stile which on our last visit had been wired over. It is a two-step planked stile, approximately 3 feet high and it is about 15 inches from the highest step over the top of the stile. Having negotiated the stile, head straight across the field up towards the gate on the other side. At the gate turn left up to the road.

When you get to the road you can see Icklesham smock mill on the hillside in front of you. Known as Hog Hill Mill it was built at Pett in 1781 and moved to this hilltop in 1790. It remained in use until 1920 and over recent years has been restored to an alternative commercial use.

3 Turn right along the lane and follow it right back until you are facing the **New Gate**. (There is an alternative footpath, but again there are issues with a couple of wired stiles. If you wish to take the footpath, turn sharp right at the lane over the stile. Keep ahead crossing the field and across two stiles at the end. Keep the tree line on your left. On your right you have wide views over Winchelsea Beach and the English Channel. This is a panorama

The 14th-century New Gate now stands isolated in the trees, far removed from the rest of the town.

not lost on the military during the Second World War as you will pass by a **concrete observation post** hidden in the treeline at the crest of the hill. Keep following the path until you reach the gate out onto the lane on your left hand side. Go through the gate and turn right back down the lane until you are facing the New Gate.)

Winchelsea was surrounded by a defensive wall and flooded ditch with four main entrance gates. Three survive and this is the smallest, being built around the year 1330. Its angled construction reflects a bend in the long-lost town walls. It is an indication of the size of the town many centuries ago that this gate is now half a mile across green fields from the nearest house in the present day town. There is a story that one devastating attack on Winchelsea only succeeded after a traitor opened this back gate to the marauding French in 1380.

4 Just before the **New Gate** there is a public footpath on your left. It is not waymarked but you just need to go through the gate on the left where there is a small passing place in the road. Keep to the right hand field boundary with the old defensive town ditch on your right hand side. Pass through the next gate in the fence on your right hand side. You now follow the footpath up the hillside (not left through the gate into the trees). Carry on up the hill to the gate, then turn left along the bridleway. At the end of the bridleway turn right along the road, a few yards later it will bear left and you will be retracing your steps back to the start point.

Rye and Camber Castle

Camber Castle in its windswept and isolated location.

A **walk in the east of the county** which takes in one of the best-preserved medieval towns in all of England. Rye is a famous tourist magnet; its heart is a maze of cobbled streets and passageways lined with all manner of ancient stone and timber frame buildings, its hill topped with a Norman church. Rye was once surrounded by the sea on three sides - our walk will cross land that was many centuries ago beneath the waves – the town's maritime heritage dates back to Norman times. It still retains some of its 13th-century defences, whilst one of the inns in the town is claimed to date back to 1189. There is also the chance to visit Camber Castle, built by Henry VIII to defend the town. The castle is a rare survivor; unlike most castles which saw continual development and evolution, it was abandoned early in its life and so retains its original design. It also welcomes dogs!

Terrain

Paths and country lanes. There are very short distances of pavement walking alongside a busy road. Parts of the walk include sections of long-distance footpaths. If you take the diversion through the town at Rye many of the streets have a harsh cobbled surface, although there are pavements which will be easier on paws.

Dog factors

Distance: 5 miles, more if you take the trip around Rye itself.
Road walking: Mostly quiet lanes, but two very short distances on the pavement alongside the main A259. Also a short distance alongside a residential road in Rye.
Livestock: Depending on the time of year there may be sheep grazing in the fields around Camber Castle.
Stiles: None.
Nearest vets: Cinque Ports Vets, Rye Veterinary Surgery, Cinque Ports Square, Rye TN31 7AN, ☎ 01797 222265

Where to park

There is plenty of on-street unrestricted parking in the old town of Winchelsea. Please park with care. **Map**: OS Explorer 125 Romney Marsh.

How to get there

From the north take the M20 through Kent to Ashford, exit at Junction 10 and follow the signs for the A2070 to Brenzett, then picking up the A259 to Hastings. The A259 will pass alongside the old town at Winchelsea. From the west follow the A259 from Hastings. **Grid Ref**: TQ904091. **Sat Nav**: TN36 4EN.

Refreshments

The Old Grain Store café on the Strand in Rye allows dogs indoors, and is situated close to point 3 on the walk. The Strand is behind the main road but before the bottom of the hill. ☎ 01797 229290. The 17th-century Ypres Castle Inn, behind the Ypres Tower in Rye, is a little bit off the main walk but right next to one of the main sights in Rye if you take the diversion into the town. It is down the steps, squeezed in between the tower and the gun garden. Dogs are welcome and there is the chance of a dog treat on the house. However, the pub does ask that dogs be kept away from children and anyone eating, and be on a lead. Open daily from 12 noon until 11 pm (later Fridays and Saturdays), serving food until 3 pm and from 6 pm excluding Sunday nights and Bank Holidays. May be closed some Mondays during the winter months. This is a popular pub with an excellent selection of real ales; don't over indulge in the 6.2% variety at lunchtime! It's worth phoning in advance if you want to eat, ☎ 01797 223248. Elsewhere in the town there is the usual variety of convenience stores.

East Sussex – A Dog Walker's Guide

The Walk

. . . .

1 From the **Strand Gate** in Winchelsea, walk down the hill. At the bottom, take the steps on the right hand side down to the main road. Cross the road (you will need to do this as there is pavement only on the other side). After a few yards where the main road turns left, keep ahead, crossing the road again and walk into **Sea Road**. Continue along Sea Road. Where the road turns 90 degrees to the right, keep going ahead along the driveway and follow it round the corner. After a few yards, the driveway continues ahead, but you need to take the track bearing right. With the farm on your right hand side, keep to the left and after a few yards pass through the gate into the fields.

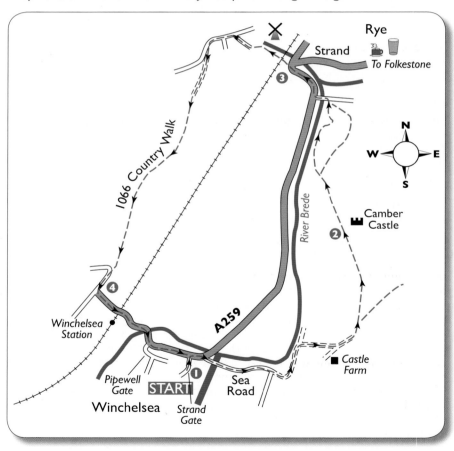

Where the rough tracks diverge, keep to the left hand track and continue along it until you reach the castle.

Camber Castle dates from 1512 when a first tower was built to protect maritime Rye from attack. Over the years the French had taken to this as a bit of a pastime, on one occasion burning most of the town to the ground and carrying off the church bells as loot. Within a few years the castle had been enlarged to become a symmetrical Tudor artillery fort, part of a chain of defences along the south coast to protect the county from invasion. However, after a hundred years the harbour area started to silt up, the sea retreated and the castle became obsolete. It was abandoned in 1637 and left to ruin until the 1970s when it was bought for the state. It is possible to visit, but the fabric of the castle means that the numbers of visitors are restricted to small groups. At the time of writing the castle is only open on summer Saturday afternoons for one guided tour each afternoon. However, it is well worth planning ahead, it's an atmospheric spot with no crowds, no tourist trappings, just the ancient castle in its isolated windswept location. The bonus for dog walkers is that, unlike many castles, dogs are welcome on the tour. Check the English Heritage website to confirm details.

2 After the castle, return to the path and continue with the fence line on your left hand side. Carry on along the path in the same direction. Keep to the left of the next water course. The path soon brings you to the **River Brede**. Follow the path along the riverbank. You will have to take a very slight detour away from the river as the path dips down and returns through a metal gate. The path emerges onto a driveway. Keep ahead for a few yards, then turn left onto the road and cross the river and turn right onto the main road. To visit Rye, follow the main road over the river – various streets leading up to the old town are accessible from behind the harbourside buildings.

In medieval times, Rye was an important trading centre and a member of the Cinque Ports confederation with a history of providing ships for the military use of the king. It was an important medieval port but like Camber Castle the sea retreated and it lost its importance. Later the town became embroiled in the smuggling trade. It is now a tourist honeypot, but it still oozes charm and there is a wealth of places of interest. If you want a walk through the best parts of the town we would suggest the following: Walk up Mermaid Street, turn right along Traders Passage up into Watchbell Street. Continue along Watchbell Street where it becomes Church Square, with the Parish Church of St Mary on the left. At the end bear right down to the Ypres Tower and the gun garden behind it. Return up to the church but follow the street around the right hand side of the church. Then turn left into Market Street and left up to the main door of the church. At the door turn right along the short footpath next to the churchyard and at the end bear right into West Street. Follow it around the corner and the next left is Mermaid Street, which

A typical quiet corner of Rye. This is West Street looking back at St Mary's church. The angle of the chimney is not an optical illusion!

will take you back down the hill to rejoin the walk. There is so much of interest in Rye to take in and see, make sure you have enough time to finish the walk!

3 To continue the walk without visiting the town, do not cross the river but instead cross the road just before the bridge and take the footpath which is now facing you, with the windmill ahead and the river on your right hand side. Cross the railway line with care, and then follow the path as it veers left. Cross the car park and turn left out onto the road. Keep going along the road for a short distance, but where the road bears slightly to the right, take the path on the left. This is part of the 1066 Country Walk which you will follow for about a mile. Above you and to the right are the old sea cliffs. Continue along the path until you reach the lane and then keep going ahead in the same direction along the lane taking the next left hand turn.

4 You now follow this lane past **Winchelsea Station** all the way back to the town which you can see in front of you. After you have crossed the river, the lane comes out at the main road. Keep going ahead and then walk up the hill passing through the ancient **Pipewell Gate** and into **North Street**. Once you are in North Street, any right hand turn will take you back to the middle of the old town.